The
Big Sell

OTHER BOOKS BY PIERRE BERTON

FAST FAST FAST FAST RELIEF (1962)

ADVENTURES OF A COLUMNIST (1960)

JUST ADD WATER AND STIR (1959)

KLONDIKE (1958)

THE MYSTERIOUS NORTH (1956)

THE GOLDEN TRAIL (1955)

THE ROYAL FAMILY (1954)

For younger readers

THE SECRET WORLD OF OG (1962)

The
Big Sell

by
Pierre Berton

An Introduction to the Black Arts of Door-to-Door
Salesmanship & Other Techniques

MCCLELLAND AND STEWART LIMITED
TORONTO/MONTREAL

The Canadian Publishers
McClelland and Stewart Limited
25 Hollinger Road, Toronto 16.

LITHOGRAPHED AND BOUND IN CANADA
BY
McCorquodale & Blades (Printers) Ltd.

Contents

To
Herbert Sussan

*Unless otherwise indicated, the names used in this book
are real*

The
Big Sell

Neverland

"Good morning, madam," said the nice young man on the doorstep. "My name is Beauregard Finch and I wish to make it clear from the outset that I am not taking a survey."

"*Amazing! Then you must be getting points for an Educational Trip to Europe.*"

"Oddly, madam, you are wrong. I am not gathering points at all. I am not working my way through medical school. I am not practicing elocution as so many young persons seem to be these days."

"*Then I know what you're doing! You are representing the advertising department of a large corporation. You want to get my opinion concerning a new product that has not yet been released through retail outlets.*"

"Perish the thought, madam. Nothing could be further from my mind."

"Then you have been recommended by a friend and you are here to show me how, by recommending MY friends, I can get an amazing new household product free of charge."

"Alas, madam, no one recommended me to you. I was dumped out of a truck down the street by the sales manager and ordered to knock on every door. So here I am at yours. I am a salesman, pure and simple. My product is an automatic can opener. I am *selling* it, not advertising it. This is *not* a special offer; it is our regular offer. There is one price: $6.95; there are no gimmicks. We cannot reduce the price because we have reached rock bottom. And I guarantee you, madam, that when you examine this can opener I shall not tell you it is an inferior can opener and that I just happen to have a much better can opener out in the car—a can opener which sells for $25.62 plus carrying charges.

"I am a salesman, pure and simple, madam. By purchasing a can opener from me you will save yourself an arduous trip to the can-opener store. That is what I offer—personal service at your door. . . ."

—From an old and
not very believable legend

4

1

The World of Make-believe

This is a book about modern fairy tales. They are, admittedly, rather commercial fairy tales since they are used to extract varying sums of money from the listeners; but they are fairy tales for all that. The characters they portray are mythical. The things these characters say and the way they act are quite unreal. Yet, as is the case with all good fairy tales, large numbers of people persist in believing them.

They are designed to catch and hold the listener's attention; what fairy tale isn't? And, in their own way, they are both entertaining and instructive, though that is not really their purpose. Their purpose is to sell.

Sometimes the things that are sold are tangible: a set of cookware; a vacuum cleaner; a Bible; a half ton of food supplement. Just as often the merchandise is more ephemeral: a dream of fame and fortune; the secret of popularity; a vision of sudden prosperity; the hope of eternal security. Sometimes, though the listener may not know it, the thing that is being sold is the tale itself and nothing more.

This book, then, deals with the black side of the great North American art of salesmanship. It deals not with the normal exaggerations and minor inconsistencies of workaday sales life on this continent but with simple deception expertly planned and ingeniously executed. It deals with a world in which things are rarely what they appear to be; in which men and women play roles and memorize their lines as carefully as any actor; in which the customer himself becomes a player, unconsciously mouthing words that have been written for him; in which the sincerest form of insincerity is ever the most successful. It is a topsy-turvy world of self-deception in which the salesman, often enough, is mesmerized along with his customers. It is a larcenous world, in which the larceny tends to be about equal on either side. It is a big-money world, involving tens of millions of dollars annually. We have all glimpsed it at one time or another, and most of us, at one time or another, have been caught up in it and even captured by it.

It differs from the normal world of sales in one other respect: its people are among the most aggressive of all, even though they may not always appear so. They do not wait behind counters for customers to stroll through the door; it is their task to go out and find the customer—by mail or by telephone or by camping on his front porch—and then to seize him by his figurative lapels and shake a sale out of him.

This kind of a salesman has three things working for him: the little bit of larceny that lurks in almost every man, the little bit of trust that is also in him, and the little bit of yearning—for a bargain or a financial windfall or a better life.

Much of the research for this book was done around the city of Toronto, Canada, and many of the examples, though not all of them, come from Toronto and its environs. Toronto, which is now the tenth largest city on the continent, is a particularly fertile field for this sort of inquiry since, through a peculiarity of circumstance, a good proportion of its citizens are among the most trusting and yearning in the land.

There are two reasons for this. First, Toronto has become one of the great immigrant cities of North America: one third of its million-and-a-half population consists of postwar European immigrants. These are people unused and unconditioned to the direct-sales methods and the mail-order and telephone techniques of this continent. At least half of them have an unfamiliarity with the language that makes the reading of a conditional sales contract's agate type a nuisance if not an impossibility; they believe what they are told; they put their faith in the friendly man on their doorstep; they are honestly bewildered when the dawn comes and it is explained to them what they have signed away with a scrawl of a proffered pen. This is equally true of the newcomers from the British Isles, who, though they can read the language, are conditioned to a world in which a man's word is considered to be his bond.

The second reason has to do with the unique nature of the ethics of Toronto's retail world. Old Toronto is a Methodist town founded on Methodist principles. Its most successful merchant was a Methodist named Timothy Eaton who invented The Store with the Money-Back Guarantee and built it into what is today the richest privately owned business on the face of the earth. What Timothy began others had to continue—or face mercantile destruction from his great retail and mail-order empire. Thus in Toronto today the money-back guarantee means more, perhaps, than in many U.S. cities. It means, no less, that a woman can order a cocktail dress from Eaton's or its largest rival, Simpsons-Sears, wear it to half a dozen parties, decide she doesn't like it, and simply pick up the phone to have it collected and returned, no questions asked, money cheerfully refunded. There is a legion of legends in Toronto about families who have kept furniture for months, women who have taken home a dozen coats and dresses on approval, hostesses who have ordered sets of dishes and glasses for parties—and then returned them later without causing a whimper of dissent. In a sense, Toronto consumers have been brainwashed into believing that everything is returnable and that when you sign a document promising to pay, you are not really signing for keeps. They are putty in the hands of those nice young men who slide a legal form under their fountain pens while whispering all the time that, if they don't like the Handy-Dandy All-Purpose Quince Parer and Toothpaste Blender, all they need to do is send it back.

Torontonians, then, are close to being ideal marks, or mooches, or eggs or suckers, in the varying argot of the trade. But, as the figures show, they are not *that* different from the rest of the continent. There is no practice described in this book which does not flourish at one time or another in every corner of the land, and which will not flourish again in the future.

2

One of the aspects of modern salesmanship, especially the fairy-tale kind, is a sort of studied insincerity which is all the more surprising because it is so often patent. So many of the intensely personal letters penned to panting prospects have quite obviously been lithographed, mimeographed, or hecto-graphed by the thousands.

Here, for instance, is a personal letter sent to me by L. J. Rosencrantz, president of National Technical Schools, a mail-order-study organization in Los Angeles, to which I once sent a coupon of inquiry.

Dear Friend:

You will remember who "L.J." is, I am sure, as you read my note.

All of our people here at National Technical Schools call me "L.J."—and even though I am the president, there is nothing "brass hat" about me. I try to be one of the "gang". . .

In writing you this time, more than ever before, I am writing to you man to man, just as a fellow might write to a friend who had failed to answer his letters . . .

I confess that I have been disappointed because, in spite of all that I have tried to do for you—in spite of the interest I tried to take in your plans—you never even took the trouble to write and tell me your reaction to my suggestions.

So, naturally enough, I feel sort of down . . .

Mr. Rosencrantz signed this man-to-man letter "Still your friend," but it would bring more of a lump to the throat if it were not so obviously churned out by an offset machine. Still, this was something of a step forward since the previous six letters from Mr. Rosencrantz and his colleagues had been merely stenciled.

An equally sincere letter was sent along to me a couple of years ago by the North American School of Conservation. I had sent a coupon inquiry to this company and had received three letters—all of them "final offers"—quoting the price of the course at $189. These letters stopped, but I then began to get letters from a similar school called The Forestry and Wildlife Course, which cost only $64.50. The latter institution sent me a copy of a personal letter that it claimed its president had received from the president of the more expensive school.

> Dear Mr. Morten:
> Enclosed you will find . . . the name and address of a young man I think you might be able to help. . . . He wrote in response to one of our ads, but in spite of an apparently sincere interest in a Conservation Career he did not enroll. . . . As you and I both know so well, the Conservation Service urgently *needs* young men with the ambition to prepare themselves in advance. I would be failing in my duty as an educator if I did not open every possible door through which this young man and the Service might get together for mutual benefit. . . .

Anybody with the ability to spot a raging forest fire at 300 paces should have been able to see that this intensely personal and public-spirited letter was Multigraphed.

Many well-known and responsible firms use similar techniques: "Your record here has won the admiration of everybody at the office," writes the Trans-Canada Credit Corporation in a form letter to a woman who has not dealt with the company for years. "As one of our loyal and valued customers you are listed as one of our PREFERRED ACCOUNTS," writes The Guild of Canada in a form letter to a woman who has never heard of them. Even the venerable Encyclopaedia Britannica sends out an *exclusive-limited-to-a-few-persons-like-yourself* brochure, dropped in the mailbox and addressed only to The Householder, yet containing a certificate "numbered and registered in your name."

One would expect that these sincerely insincere letters

would raise the level of the public cynicism regarding all sales methods. It is possible that they have. Yet the fact that they are churned out by the millions and that they actually do bring results suggests that we are by no means a continent of 100 per cent doubters. What is happening, really, is that phony sincerity is now recognized and accepted as a legitimate sales tool. Though this may serve to blur and confuse the accepted values, it is generally conceded to be an Okay Thing if it can be shown that it works; and it does work.

I am told by an ex-salesman, for instance, that real sincerity is frowned on in the door-to-door Bible sales field. The firms that distribute these expensive Bibles, at $35 to $50 a volume, originally felt that devout Christians would be the best people to sell the Good Book. This turned out to be disastrous since the real Christians ended up giving their Bibles away in a commendable attempt to proselytize. The best Bible salesmen turned out to be dyed-in-the-wool heathens who were cynical enough and clever enough to out-Christian the Christians when they got their feet in the nation's doorways.

Such salesmen tend to have a godlike appearance; but if the light of divine truth shines from their eyes, their chief quality is an ability to extract hard cash from the anointed. To help them, they use a set of instructions called "Overcoming Objections," which has been found to be sure-fire. I quote a smattering here, to give the general flavor of the approach. Their sincerity is unquestionable. So is the pragmatism of the company's instructions, which are capitalized and bracketed at the appropriate points.

If the customer hesitates about buying, the salesman says: "You know, Mrs. Jones, a Bible can't be sold to anyone. When a person purchases a Bible some Power higher than man is leading him. The only advice I can give you is to let your conscience be your guide. You know, our conscience is the Voice of God speaking to us, and it never tells us wrong. Your conscience is telling you what to do now. Just listen to it: (*Instructions:* CLOSE THE SALE NOW) I feel your conscience will never bother you for purchasing a wonderful Bible like this because no grief ever comes from doing good, isn't that true?" (*Instructions:* PRODUCE PAD AND PENCIL)

If the housewife says she cannot afford a $35 or $50 Bible, the salesman has several ready answers. Here is one:

"You know, Mrs. Jones, our Blessed Saviour provides us with food, clothing, home, shelter and everything else we have on earth. He is not, however, as concerned with material things as He is with spiritual things. (NOW CLOSE) Surely we believe that since Jesus provides us with all of these other things, He will surely provide the way for us to have the very best Holy Bible, if we are sincere and really want it. You believe that, don't you? I was sure you did." (PAD AND PENCIL)

If the housewife says "Not now," the salesman says:

"You know, Mrs. Jones, if we go through life saying 'Not now' to spiritual things we would also like to say 'Not now' at the hour of death. If we do everything within our power here on earth to know and understand the Word of God, we can, instead, smile and say: 'Now, Lord, I am ready.' (NOW CLOSE) If when we reach the end of the trail we can say: 'Now I am ready,' certainly our life has been a grand success. We all believe that, don't we?" (PAD AND PENCIL)

If a housewife says she already has several nice Bibles, the salesman is instructed to say:

"Oh, I know that, Mrs. Jones; in fact, I would be just a little fearful about coming into your home if I felt you had no Bibles here. Thank God we seldom find homes any more that don't have Bibles of some kind. Just think, though, Mrs.

12

Jones, how much more beautiful and understandable this Masterpiece is. (NOW CLOSE) Why, if it didn't do more than one thing and that was to give you, your good husband, or one of your loved ones just a little more appreciation and a little better understanding of the Teachings of Christ, it would be worth its weight in gold. You believe that, don't you?" (PAD AND PENCIL)

One of the problems all salesmen have is customers who just stand there and say nothing. "We must force some comments or some objections," the Bible salesmen are told. For instance, the salesman may say:

"Not long ago, Mrs. Jones, a lady from Richmond, Va., wrote our company the saddest and most beautiful letter I have ever read. She told us about a horrible accident in which her youngest child, a lad only seven years old, was critically injured. She said that during the long hours she and her husband sat by his bedside they both learned what the Bible meant by the valley of the shadow of death; but they had His rod and His staff there to comfort them in the form of this wonderful Bible. As if by a miracle, their son recovered. (NOW CLOSE) Every mother and father could be proud and certainly would be blessed by having this beautiful Bible as the most important thing in their homes. Don't you agree? (HESITATE) Well, fine, you shall certainly have it." (PAD AND PENCIL)

A great deal of attention is paid to the matter of all-cash sales. A salesman, told that the household already has several Bibles, may use this prepared speech as a lever:

"We love to call on people who have nice Bibles because that shows us that we are talking to people who really love the Word of God. Such people never pass up any Bible that helps them get more knowledge of spiritual things. (NOW CLOSE) People like that usually pay cash so that others may get one on the honor plan. Wouldn't it be possible for you to finish it all up by paying cash today?"

If a housewife says she can't pay cash and doesn't buy on credit, the salesman says:

"That's very good, Mrs. Jones, as far as most things are concerned. You know, however, that you cannot go down to the water company and buy your water supply for the next five years. Every home buys its water on a month-to-month basis; the same is true of gas bills, other public utilities, even income taxes. Let's take your electric lights, for instance. Ordinarily, you pay for your electric light on a month-to-month basis. (NOW CLOSE) The Bible is the Light of the World. It is a Heavenly light and surely much more important than mere electric lights. That is certainly true, isn't it, Mrs. Jones?" (PAD AND PENCIL)

And if Mrs. Jones says she doesn't even have the down payment, the salesman is trained to say this:

"I'm sure you'll find that one of your good neighbors or even your grocer will be happy to loan you the small amount required as a down payment, especially since you are using the money to get one of these lovely Bibles."

Salesmen are taught that the "close" is the most important part of the sale. This is simply a statement or question designed to get a favorable answer from the potential customer, worded in such a way that the favorable answer also constitutes a commitment to buy. "Throw that close!" says the Bible sales instruction pamphlet, slipping momentarily into a sportier jargon.

And what happens if the customer cannot keep up her Bible payments? Why, the Christian company that sells the Bible sends another Christian around to repossess the Good Book, as it would a used car or TV set. No doubt this Christian also feels that a Higher Power is leading him—such as the finance company.

3

What kind of people are these men whose creed is the quick close and the blitz sale, and whose tools are the handy pen, the conditional sales contract, and the sincere story? Here is a former member of the breed, now in charge of international sales for a large encyclopaedia firm, describing his fellows:

"The specialty salesman is a very interesting man because every one that I've ever met is a neurotic in some way or another. The stable, responsible, well-adjusted guy gets out of school and either he has an idea of what he would like to do or he goes out to seek a job and he finds a job. He's stable. He brings home so much money every week. He knows how to live on it and he saves a little, or maybe he doesn't save a little, but he knows how much money he's got coming in.

"The specialty salesman is a guy with a severe inferiority complex. He blisters and he blusters and he tells everybody how great he is, but he's really very insufficient to the task of living. He fears that if he went into a company and had to compete against other men, he could never get anywhere and he'd wind up exactly where he started. He's afraid of this terrible mediocrity, so he looks around and asks himself: 'Where can I make success easy?' To him success means the prestige symbols: money, a big house, a big car. The big car especially is essential.

"So he sees an ad, and answers it. Usually it leads to a hotel room, and the manager of the company that placed the ad sits there, and generally this manager is half-starved to death himself and very neurotic and he tells the would-be salesman how Ed made $5,000 last week, or he picks another fictitious figure and tells the prospect how much money *he* made; and he holds up this big star for the poor neurotic to shoot at and he tempts him into the business.

"The salesman himself is really a nice guy. I haven't met very many men who come into this business who are not real nice guys, but they are terribly afraid of life and afraid that they can't succeed. Incidentally, they are usually accident prone. The specialty salesman is so convinced that he's nobody anyway that as soon as he starts knowing some success he steps on his own feet. He does something to prevent his own success. And he's always a guy who spends more money than he makes and, if he's making too much, he finds reasons why he can't go to work."

These salesmen, in short, bear a remarkable similarity to many of their customers; and that is not surprising since one of the new and proven sales techniques is to pretend to make a salesman out of a customer in order to sell him something. One of the methods used to attract a new salesman is to use on him the same form of deception that he himself will later use on his prospects.

In the spring of 1962, for example, one of my newspaper readers received a post card in the mail which read: "DID YOU NOTICE THIS ADVERTISEMENT IN YOUR PAPER?" The advertisement had asked for a man of between forty-five and sixty, "neat and conscientious," who owned a car and wanted to earn "up to $14,500 a year."

The post card went on to state that "I'm looking for a man in your community . . . sincere, honest, capable. . . . At the moment I haven't found that man. But if the information I have is correct, YOU are interested. . . ."

I asked a friend, who has absolutely none of the qualifications for salesmanship, to answer the post card. He mailed the attached Business Reply Card asking the Texas Refinery Corporation of Canada Ltd. to "please RUSH me complete details of this position now open in my area."

Apparently the job was not yet filled, because within a

week he received two thick envelopes in the mail from Fort Worth, Texas. Both contained lengthy form letters.

Form Letter No. 1, which arrived first by airmail, announced that it had been written after Form Letter No. 2, which was being sent by ordinary mail. In it, Mr. A. B. Canning, the president, explained that, "after mailing the first letter, the thought came to me that you might like to find out something about our company and to get complete details of our sales proposition as quickly as possible." After the thought came to him, Mr. Canning apparently had the letter, complete with his signature, run off on the Multilith machine so he could have several thousand copies for his files.

Both letters enclosed an application form for screening prospective salesmen for the job. The job involved selling Mightyplate Asbestos Roof Coating on commission to businessmen. "You may be just that particular red-blooded Sales Advisor we need," Mr. Canning wrote. "So let's find out."

My spy cheerfully filled in the application form. His qualifications, it seemed to me, were lamentable. He made it clear that he had absolutely no sales experience. He listed his age as ten years below the minimum asked for on the post card. He gave answers to the psychological questions which revealed him to be the exact opposite of the gregarious, likable types usually selected for direct-sales work; and he suggested by his answers that he was virtually broke, improvident, and not very neat.

What did he enjoy most—meeting and talking to people . . . tinkering about the house . . . or gardening? Tinkering, said the spy. *What was his favorite recreation—spending a quiet evening with family . . . going out with friends . . . or attending a club party?* Quiet evening, wrote the spy. *Did he find it simple, fairly easy, or difficult to strike up a conversation with a total stranger?* Difficult, the spy indicated. *Did he like to attend championship sports events?* NO; the spy preferred staying home with his hobbies. Then he showed that he had very little insurance, no savings, meager possessions, and preferred to go around without a coat or tie—hardly a sincere, live-wire salesman.

As he was completing his application form another letter arrived in which Mr. Canning said: "I still feel you MAY be the man capable of filling our sales vacancy and earning yourself $15,000 a year—or even $25,000."

"I say this," Mr. Canning continued, "because I assume you to be a mature, honorable, warm-natured type of man who likes people! That you are a man who has had a reasonable amount of sales or business experience. That's the type of man who succeeds and prospers with us."

My friend thought of cheating a bit on his application but decided against it, in spite of this letter. He did cheat on his references, however: two previous places of employment he listed were phonies. He mailed in the form, but he did not expect too much from Texas Refinery Corp.

A week later, an airmail letter arrived from Mr. Canning, saying his application form had come in and "it enables me to make an immediate survey of your background and qualifications." My friend's heart sank, but then rose a bit as he read on: "On the surface they look just fine. Everything seems to indicate that you're fully qualified to do mighty well in our Line."

But then—more gloom:

"Please bear in mind, however, that in order to maintain the reputation of our Sales force as one of the finest in Canada, it's necessary to make a rather extensive analysis and a careful investigation of all applicants. Ordinarily this doesn't take very long. But in some cases a few days are required to secure the necessary information. Nevertheless, every effort is being made to rush your investigation as much as possible. And we'll express our sincere judgment the moment it's concluded."

My friend realized that if the corporation checked his references or his previous places of employment, it would discover he was not what he claimed to be. This was made quite clear in the letter:

"Our Organization . . . [is] composed of the most admirable sort of men—men of character . . . and honor . . . of patriotism . . . of humility . . . of tact . . . and many other virtues! Practically all of our men are mature family men who love liberty and freedom and believe in good honest effort. They believe it's their duty as red-blooded, virile patriots to provide good livings and some of the comforts of life for their families. . . . I hope very much our check-up shows you to be just such a man. And your APPLICATION form leads me to believe that it will!"

My friend had a feeling the check-up would reveal him as an impoverished introvert and therefore, by definition, unpatriotic.

Nonetheless, a week later, the happy news arrived: "Welcome to our organization. Your application for a Sales Connection with us has been approved. Hence you are now a Texas Refinery Corp. 'Advisor' . . . ." There followed several Multigraphed pages and then these closing words: "Our check-up covering you was quite thorough and complete. It indicates rather conclusively to me that you have the attributes that should enable you to make this work pay for you. . . ."

As far as we were able to determine, the Texas Refinery Corp. had made no effort, at that point, to check up on any aspect of my man's background. But, no doubt, in its relentless hunt for good commission men it has developed its own secret system for separating the chaff from the wheat.

This automatic series of form letters suggests the psychological kinship between salesman and customer in certain fields. I once had an extended conversation with another of the breed, an aluminum-window salesman who had spent six years knocking on doors. He was trying to kick the habit and he found it hard to do. He was a good-looking, stocky, horn-rimmed, crew-cut, neatly tailored twenty-three-year-old who looked closer to twenty-nine. He talked easily, even when discussing his own problems, and there was a certain dynamic quality about him that compelled attention:

"Each of us suffers from a basic insecurity which he can't shake. It comes from the lack of goal in our business. Everybody wants some kind of a goal, but there's none for us. There's nothing solid to live by. There's no reward aside from monetary gain. That's why each of us has some kind of outlet—liquor, girls, fast cars, fancy clothes. With me it was trips to L.A.; trips to Cuba; trips to Miami. For me the outlet always came when I got back into town with a suntan and a new suit and snapped my fingers and told the boys how I blew a few hundred at Vegas.

"You won't believe this, but I used to go nuts if I didn't have a minimum of $100 cash in my pocket. You don't know the feeling that I'd have if that roll dropped below $100. If I was five dollars under, I'd go straight to the bank and get more. I guess it was a sign of security to be able to peel some bills off a big roll at a night club or a restaurant."

This man had started at the age of seventeen taking color photographs in the home. He quickly learned the kind of fast sales pitch that persuaded gullible mothers to buy three pictures for $27: "The samples were wonderful," he said, "but the color faded in about two weeks."

He rose swiftly to crew manager and began recruiting other salesmen. Here he learned the axiom: "You can take advantage of people, or else you can take advantage of peo-

ple who want to take advantage of people." He told prospective salesmen they could easily make $200 a week in com-
missions, and he found that they believed him because so
many salesmen are themselves suckers at heart. They believe
because it is their business to believe; it makes it easier to
seem sincere.

He had run the gamut of door-to-door merchandise, had
this salesman—accident insurance . . . water softeners
. . . aluminum windows. He paid $24 for his windows and
sold them for $60, which meant that on a set of eight he
would make almost $300 net profit:

"Just think of it—sixty bucks apiece for a lousy aluminum
window you could pick up at Eaton's for fifteen or twenty
bucks. Yet they went for them—imagine!" (And he showed
his contempt for the customer.) "The people who bought
them, they just don't know which end is up. They're not like
people at all; they're yokels; they live like they're in a dream;
you tell them anything, they'll swallow it."

So he told them he was the boss's son driving up in his
shiny Pontiac convertible and about to open a new branch
office in the district. And he was preceded by a front man
who knocked on the door first and said that his employer required three or four lovely homes to help create interest in
future business—and if they would only allow his company
to put some sample windows for display purposes on this
lovely, gracious old-world home, why, the company would
pay them $10 for every sale that was made as a result of their
recommendation.

"I tell you we cleaned up through Northern Ontario. We
put aluminum windows on shacks even!—on houses that
were leaning over or falling down—rotten farm houses top-
pling to pieces—on sheds, on outhouses, on everything. Just
flatter them and offer them money and they'd fall for the
story."

I need your help, Mr. Jones, and for that reason I'm pre-

*pared to make every allowance as far as price is concerned.
I'll go right off the cost sheet for you. I'm not a salesman.
My father owns the company. In the event an unexpected
bill arose and you're stuck for payment, you would get in
touch with me, wouldn't you? I'll gladly extend you over.*

And the boss's son who was not the boss's son would study
the prospect shrewdly, mentally reckoning the financial
lengths to which he could be driven. Then he would tie him
to a contract as binding as a mortgage and drive off to the
next shack down the road. Sometimes he would not bother
to show a sample; he sold on the story alone.

"Look at your windows!" he'd say. "They're rotten!" And
he'd pull off a piece of the old sash. "Tell you what I'll do:
I'll throw in a new frame for free." And he would, too: four
slabs of wood nailed together and an aluminum window
jammed inside—a window that wouldn't always open.

"I'd never seen an aluminum window before in my life, but
I made $825 the first week," he told me.

And yet he quit, as he quit all his jobs, because it was getting him nowhere. There was no goal in view. The road on
which he traveled led on and on past a hundred thousand
doorsteps; but it was a road that had no end.

4

There is a curious obliqueness to certain forms of modern
salesmanship that frustrates direct inquiry. It is, for instance,
almost impossible to stop one of the fairy tales in the middle.
I have talked to people who have tried to buy a product before the sales talk was finished. "Never mind all that," they'd
say. "It looks like a pretty good vacuum cleaner. I'll take it."
When this happens the salesman is apt to give his customer

a half-hurt, half-baffled look. It is something he is not used to. He doesn't quite know how to proceed. He would much prefer to go on to the end, using the careful conversational devices in which he has been trained, asking the prescribed questions and getting the expected answers, and not producing the pen and the contract until the proper moment. I have been told of cases in which a salesman, cut off in the middle of his story, has closed the deal and then insisted on finishing the rest of the talk anyway.

It is very difficult, for instance, to buy an encyclopaedia directly over the phone, simply by calling up and asking for the price. No matter what you do, most of the companies seem to want to send a salesman around to your door to go through the entire one-hour talk. The fairy tale is part of the sale price, and the companies insist in giving value for the money.

This obliqueness of attitude translates itself in various ways, but never so revealingly, perhaps, as in the advertisements for sales help placed in the classified columns by many of the companies involved in the hard, direct sell. One needs a translation guide, sometimes, to understand all the euphemisms now being employed to hide that awful word "salesman."

CHOSEN applicant to be trained in special field of family service. This position offers prestige and security, sound income (on commission). Profit-sharing nation-wide organization. Applicants must be neat in appearance. Personal interview only. (Phone number)

TRANSLATION: This is an ad for salesmen to sell cemetery plots for Resthaven Memorial Gardens, door to door, high pressure.

$475
GUARANTEED SALARY
PROMOTIONAL aspects will appeal to mature men who know the price of success and are willing to pay for it. Adult educational program, new to Canada and strongly financed by parent company.
FOR appointment call personnel manager (Phone number)

TRANSLATION: You will be selling "Great Books of the Western World" door to door. "Adult education program" almost always means encyclopaedias or books of some kind. The odds are you will not get a guaranteed salary but will be paid straight commissions depending on how many sales you make.[1]

---

2 YOUNG MEN, 16–22
To assist office manager of national publishing company. Salary. Miss Francis (Phone number)

TRANSLATION: You will be selling magazine subscriptions door to door. You will not find that out by phoning, however.

[1] The phrase "guaranteed salary" in advertisements for salesmen has become almost meaningless. In 1959 the following advertisement appeared in the classified sections of Toronto newspapers:

> $12,500 PER ANNUM GUARANTEED ON SALARY AND BONUS
> We want an executive salesman for field representative in Toronto to service present accounts and to enlist new members for Canada's oldest and largest retail association.

Those who answered this ad found that it, too, did not deliver what it promised. The pay was actually $50 a week, plus $10 commission for each new client signed up, with no guarantee of anything.

The ad was placed by the Retail Merchants' Association, which that very month had been conducting a campaign against dishonest and misleading advertising.

When one of my agents phoned this number, he was told his duties would be typing. When he went to the office, he was sent out to sell magazines. Nothing was said about salary.

MEN AND WOMEN
Full Or Part Time
TO DO TELEPHONE SURVEY WORK
SALARY AND BONUS
(Phone number)

TRANSLATION: You will be making appointments for salesmen to call on prospects to sell them storm windows. The word used on the phone during this so-called "survey" will not be aluminum storm windows; you will talk about "health-giving products."

---

10 young men to do interview work in Public Relations Dept. of large publishing concern.

TRANSLATION: we want salesmen to peddle Collier's Encyclopaedia from door to door.

DUE to expansion, leading food products corporation with offices in principal cities requires several clean-cut men to train as Driver Salesmen to cover established routes.

TRANSLATION: International Health Products, Inc., wants door-to-door salesmen to sell mixing machines to housewives while pretending to introduce an economy line of powdered milk.

Such advertisements are understandable in a profession which thrives on euphemisms. A sales contract is described as a "guarantee"; a magazine is always a "journal" (when it is mentioned at all); merchandise is "placed" but never sold; customers pay nothing: they "handle" the plan; your signature on a non-cancelable contract is "for your protection"; and a salesman is never, never, *never* a salesman.

A man who took a salesman's course conducted by the Grolier Society, to learn to sell *The Book of Knowledge* door-to-door, once told me of an amusing incident in a class. The prospective salesmen were told to act out little dramas, with one man playing an angry housewife and the other a persistent encyclopaedia salesman. My man flunked his first trial when the teacher, in the role of the housewife, suddenly asked: "Are you a salesman?"

STUDENT: Well, actually I am, but . . .
TEACHER: NO! NO! NO! *Never* say you're a salesman. Now let's try it again. This time I'll be the salesman and you be the housewife. Okay; I'm knocking on the door. *Good* morning, ma'am. . . .
STUDENT: Just a moment; are you a salesman?
TEACHER: Madame, I am not here to sell you anything. As a matter of fact, if I were a salesman I'd starve to death. Actually, I'm taking a survey.

The Disinterested Surveyor is a favorite disguise in the world of the big sell. Indeed, the role has been used so often that it has worn a little thin (and bona fide survey companies are having difficulty completing their sampling as a result). A more recent and more effective disguise has been that of the Friendly Advisor.

"Good morning, Mrs. Worsely. I am from the Comprehensive Family Security Counsellor Division of Archmount Memorial Service Ltd. This department has been newly formed because of the very large number of families who, when they have had a death in their family, have turned to us for advice and guidance in connection with the many problems that arise in making final arrangements for a loved one. . . ."

This man was peddling prepaid funeral plans, and the pitch that followed was designed to flatter the subject into thinking he had been especially selected to participate in a real bargain offer. Actually, it was considerably more expensive than regulation funerals in the same city.

A third disguise is that of the Enrollment Officer who wants to make a searching inquiry to see if you are eligible for the exclusive club to which you have been nominated. In 1961, for instance, young married couples in Canada began receiving in the mail a beautifully engraved card. The gold lettering informed them that they had recently "been nominated to membership in the Young Parents' League of Canada" and that "one of our Enrollment Officers on the nominating committee will be contacting you in the next few days to explain the functions of the League or reject your nomination according to your wishes."

One prospective member reported this brief conversation when the Enrollment Officer dropped around:

ENROLLMENT OFFICER: Good evening, I am here to explain to you that membership in the League is only made possible by one member nominating another. We assume that one of your friends who is a member feels that as young parents you are deeply concerned with the welfare of your children and would be interested in becoming members of the League.

YOUNG PARENT: What are you selling?
ENROLLMENT Just give me half an hour of your
OFFICER: time. . . .
YOUNG PARENT: No! (*Slams door*)

What he was selling was $210 worth of child-guidance books for the General Reference Research Company. Yet it is quite possible that he genuinely believed himself to be an enrollment officer and not a salesman, and it is fairly certain that, when his friends asked him what he did for a living, he reported proudly that he was an Enrollment Officer for the Young Parents' League of Canada. There is a certain amount of self-mesmerization here. After talking to the practitioners of the big sell and reading some of their literature, one is led to the conclusion that large numbers of them operate by a weird kind of double-think, which makes it possible for them to believe everything they are saying, yet, at the same time, to understand that it isn't true. This is the only possible interpretation that can be placed on the printed instructions given to telephone solicitors by a firm called International Health Products of Canada, whose sales pitch, described later in this book, is one of the more deceptive I have studied.

Telephone Solicitation

Your approach over the phone should be . . . very, very friendly. . . . Make them think: "Gee, she has a friendly, pleasant voice!"

Remember always, the people you are calling have been called before—*plenty!* And they have heard most of the gimmick stories and tall tales—they know the "free" dancing lessons they have won—they know all about the "special" discounts they are being "selected" to receive—and believe me, they are fed up to the teeth with false statements—misleading claims, and out-and-out lies, to get a few minutes of their time in order to "pressure" them into a phone demonstration of some product.

We therefore must be *different* by *telling the truth* always. Naturally you can't tell everything about our program over the phone or our counsellor will have nothing to talk about when he gets there.

Every good story must have some mystery, enthusiasm, pathos, humor, and a good ending acceptable to most people, and most important of all, it must have *interest* for each particular person.

It is a *fact* that your story is only important and worth listening to if it tells each individual something that will benefit him or her.

IMPORTANT—Think of it from her viewpoint and how it will benefit her at all times, and you can't fail to gain her full attention. . . .

We are one great team of which the telephone solicitor is a main cog—you will only make money if the salesman has a good appointment which will end in him making a sale *for you!* We *want* you to make money, lots of it, so if you work and make calls you can make whatever amount you want to make. . . .

It is intriguing to note in this curious document that, as soon as the business of money is mentioned, the "counsellor" suddenly becomes a salesman again. It is even more intriguing to realize that the telephone pitch these girls were given to read contained most of the stock snares against which they were specifically warned. The final instructions were the bluntest of all.

If they say: "Are you selling this item," *answer:* "NO, we are not selling anything, Mrs. Blank, we are on a research program. . . . We won't try to *sell* you *anything*—that I promise!"

I have no doubt that many a young housewife, earning a few extra dollars as a telephone solicitor, believed implicitly in everything she was told, contradictions and all, since it is an axiom in selling that you must have faith in the product. The analogy with religion is too obvious to be labored, but it makes more understandable the fervent evangelism which accompanies so much direct salesmanship.

5

In the world of the big sell, the customer is held in no more regard by the salesman than the salesman is held by the customer. They are engaged in a running battle of wits, and if the salesman is a "shark" to his prey, the prey is variously a *mooch*, an *egg*, a *sucker*, a *mark*, or a *peasant*. These are all terms which suggest contempt; they are the salesman's and the con man's equivalent of the word *square*.

I was given one day, in a darkened bar, a postgraduate course in the art of being a mooch, from an expert on mooches. His name was Harry and I met him through a mutual friend. He did not call himself a salesman nor yet a sales representative nor even a field representative; he called himself a con man. In this, too, he was suffering from self-delusion since the select society of bona fide confidence men would not admit him to their circle; his methods were too crude, and besides, he actually did sell the customer a little something. The classic con games, which will be described in a following chapter, are not designed to sell; they are designed to take. The basic principles, however, are always the same: the larceny and the ego of the customer are the twin human frailties that must be played upon.

Harry, when I talked to him, was going back into the

paving racket, because, he said, almost everybody is a sucker for the paving racket. It was a better racket, he said, than the chimney racket, in which he considered himself the world's leading expert.

The chimney racket worked this way:

Harry would drive up to a doorway in a panel truck on which was lettered an imposing name such as ELITE CHIMNEY REPAIR. "My company is checking all the chimneys in the area," he would say to the man at the door (or, as was more often the case, the widow at the door since widows are a prime target in the chimney-repair racket). "We'd just like to make sure yours is okay. There's absolutely no charge for the service."

As Harry said, the mooch cannot resist getting something for nothing. If it's free, he'll usually say, "go ahead." "And once you've got the ladder up," said Harry, "you're in."

It was Harry's purpose to prove to the mooch that his chimney was in a state of imminent collapse. He found it easiest, he told me, to swindle professional people of considerable intelligence. "They won't come down to your level," he explained. "They have to pretend they know everything."

Harry offered them that chance:

"Looks to me like the cledes under the inner rim aren't in very good shape," he would say, squinting professionally at the chimney. He had long known that a real mooch cannot bring himself to ask what a "clede" is. The mooch would nod sagely and ask Harry to take a look.

Harry would scamper up the ladder and jimmy a few bricks off the chimney. He prided himself on partially destroying any chimney he inspected—knocking the bricks loose and actually smashing them and then forcing the whole top of the chimney off with a crowbar. He would stay on the roof for some time, bustling about and tapping and peering down inside and smashing the occasional brick; then he would hustle back down the ladder.

"We were right," he would tell the mooch. "Those cledes are in terrible shape. Rusted right down to the hones. That could be dangerous—it's against fire regulations, as you know. The inner greels have pretty well had it, owing to smoke deterioration, but I think we can save the supporting skrims, the upper ones anyway, though the faces are badly tarnished. They may have to be burnished."

The intelligent mooch would nod knowingly as Harry fed him this gobbledygook.

"Come on up the ladder and see for yourself," Harry would say, shaking the ladder a little.

Nine times out of ten, said Harry, the nervous mooch would decline to mount the ladder. He would say that he preferred to leave it all to Harry; how much would it all cost? Not too much, Harry would tell him. He would know better when he got on with the job; a couple of hundred dollars at the most.

From then on, Harry would have the mooch in the palm of his hand. He would keep coming down to tell him things: just as he thought, the skrims would have to be burnished; that was going to add something to the cost. Harry could judge how much the traffic would bear, and he was generally right. Usually the sum came to about $1,000.

He insisted to me that he had once taken $3,000 from a prominent family simply for fixing the eavestrough on their home.

"They'll need to be leaded inside and out," he told the woman of the house, "but once they're leaded they'll last a lifetime." Then he painted them with ordinary red paint.

He is a psychologist, of course. Grouches are his meat. If he is warned away from a certain house by a colleague, he will attack the front door head on as a matter of pride. If the mooch gets rough, Harry will simply say: "Boy, they told me you were a grouch, and they were so right! It's not worth doing business with you." Half the time, said Harry, he will get called back, and when that happens the mooch is properly trapped.

The paving racket, which Harry has since been engaged in, works this way:

He and his partner purchase a truck worth about $12,000. They make a down payment of $1,500 and drive it away (for they are adept at cozening car dealers, too). Then they go to the nearest paving company and hire as many men as they need simply by offering them better wages. They can afford to do this because they earn much more for paving driveways than legitimate firms do.

They buy cheap crankcase oil and other paving materials. They paint a company name on their truck; *any* name. The company isn't registered. Its phone number and address—if it has one at all—keep changing. The name itself changes every two weeks as Harry and his gang move swiftly from town to town. Thus, it is almost impossible for enraged householders to track them down. If they do, all they can launch is a civil suit. The chimney racket is out-and-out criminal fraud, but in the paving racket Harry has actually performed a service, albeit shoddy and expensive. You can sue him, if you can catch him, but he won't go to jail.

What he does is to charge outrageous prices—two or three times the going rate—for a job that will not last six months. At the end of the season he stops making payments on the truck, turns it in, and vanishes with his profit.

The mooches who listen to his smooth talk always believe that they are getting a bargain.

"Look," said Harry one day to an intelligent mooch, "because it's for you, I'm going to knock $50 off my price, but for God's sake don't tell anybody; I'd be out of business in a

33

week at that rate!" And the two of them smiled a conspira-
torical smile. Harry says he felt pleased about this because
the man was a highly placed penal official. He paid $700 for
a $290 job, the same as everybody else.

"But why are you telling me all this?" I asked Harry, after
he had explained it. "You know I'll print it. Won't that hurt
you?"

"Not a bit," said he. "I'll even clip what you write and
show it to the mooches. *Look at this,* I'll say, shaking my
head, *isn't it awful what these fly-by-nights are doing? Why,
they're ruining the business for legitimate corporations such
as the one I represent.* And then I'll explain how much lower
my prices are and how ironclad my guarantee is. There'll be
no trouble."

Harry's experiences with mooches who believe they are
forcing down his prices supports the theory of my friend
Buddy Abrahams that "the big gimmick in specialty selling
is to appeal to the larceny of the customer." That is why so
many sales today are disguised as private sales; the customer
thinks he can get the better of a bargain if he is dealing
with a nonprofessional. The newspapers, for instance, are full
of advertisements for automobiles, furniture, rugs, electric
ranges, and automatic washers, all of which seem to be for
sale at a sacrifice by a private owner. I know of one man who
consistently advertises various appliances for sale from his
home, always at a "sacrifice." He is, in effect, an appliance
dealer; but the prospects don't know this. When they phone
they are told his mother-in-law is moving in with him; she
has brought along an extra automatic washer, which he
must dispose of. His mother-in-law has been moving in with
him for several years, but the customers are convinced that
they are stealing him blind. They offer him $75 for a ten-
year-old automatic washer that isn't worth $20, in the belief

that they are getting a hot bargain on a recent model. He takes their money cheerfully.

Not far away there is a motherly little woman who uses a similar stratagem to sell furniture and rugs. *Bedroom suite, like new; private,* her advertisements read; and the mooches come flocking. Her story is that her mother has decided to move out and she wants to get rid of the suite to make room for the new baby. Her home is crammed with such suites. Another motherly little woman advertises sacrifices on chesterfields and rugs "one month old, never used." I once studied her ads over the period of a month and estimated that she was spending $2,400 a year in the classified sections. Her story is that her daughter has just bought a house, that the mortgage rate is too high, that she has had to cancel the deal and mama is stuck with the extra furniture. I sent somebody out to look over her place one day and discovered that there were a dozen new rugs stacked in her hallway. Various larcenous mooches buy them over the phone in the belief that they are getting the better of the motherly little woman; they would save money if they bought the rugs in a rug shop.

The car dealers, of course, have understood the private-sale technique for years and used it to their advantage. A good proportion of the ads for used cars that appear to be private sales are actually inserted by dealers who operate from their homes. The stories are always ingenious. *The wife doesn't like the color of this car; you know how women are; I've just got to get rid of it and take a beating. . . . My daughter bought this and lost her job and now I'm stuck with the payments; for God's sake do me a favor, Mac, and take it off my hands; I'll let it go for cost. . . . I got a new job in Vancouver and I can't fool around bargaining; the car has to go; it's yours at a sacrifice.* I have checked out dozens of license numbers on these so-called "private sales." About one in three turned out to be owned by a car lot. But the mooch is always convinced that he has got himself a live mooch of his own to work his will on; when he is in this kind of a mood, the mooch is a mooch indeed.

The car dealers' methods of handling mooches have been more or less codified by a Hollywood sales consultant named Bob Ringer, whose techniques and sales ideas have been widely adopted. One of Ringer's psychological devices is what he calls the highball-lowball technique in which a salesman alternately offers the moon to the mooch and then offers almost nothing.

In taking in the old car, *don't appraise it!* Stop kicking their car around. He knows better than you it's a sled! Fall in love with every single car that hits your curb for appraisal: "WOW! This is the very car we need. What a break . . . I've been looking high and low just for a car like this." This is your first highball. . . . "Of course, the car is worth six (lowball), *but that doesn't mean a darned thing because I'm in a spot and I've got to have your car if I have to go to twenty grand"*. . . (This is the highball again.) If he still presses for a figure, hand him a pencil and tell him to fill THAT part of the order himself.

As every car salesman knows, there is a certain point at which the customer suddenly gives up. Lured by the prospect of a bargain, alternately promised a high price and then a low one, he suddenly caves in and signs.

Another of Ringer's sales tools involves the "closing room." This is the small glass-walled office where the car salesman does his real work, persuading the customer to sign for a car at a certain price and then returning to report that the sales manager will not allow him to close the deal at such a low amount. Says Ringer:

Never take a man into a closing room until *he's shaking all over for a particular car you've definitely settled on.* If you can get him drooling for it, he's twenty times easier to close. Paint a picture of him actually *owning* the car. Put on a show. It sells cars.

Ringer emphasizes the psychological and financial importance of a fast close.

Speed Closing is the secret. A fast deal is a fat deal. The longer a deal hangs up in the closing room, the skinnier it gets. . . . Figure all deals in round numbers. Clean up the order later. . . . Don't tell a man a new car costs $3,000. It costs twenty bucks a week. Show him that the money he throws away each month would buy a new car. *Always talk in peanuts when you sell.*

Ringer has a series of stock answers to stock remarks by timid customers who aren't sure whether they want a car or not. If a customer says he's "just looking," a salesman who has memorized the Ringer technique will propel him to a new Super Mark III and cry: "Well, here's something to look at." If a customer says he wants to talk it over with his wife, a Ringer man will "highball" him by quoting an impossibly low price in order to get him to bring his wife into the showroom.

Here are some other stock sales answers:

"I can't afford it." This is generally used if the salesman hasn't done a complete enough job of selling. Think about his hobby in the basement. Money is no object if he is DROOLING enough about the new car. An automobile is a very easy thing to turn into an obsession!

"I want an appraisal." Give him every courtesy. Give him a good appraisal, then tell him that when he's REALLY ready to deal you'll blow that figure out of the

tub. Burn him good with a big highball when he leaves and take him off the market till you get another crack at him.

(Translated, this means the customer discovers he cannot get a better price for his old car than the one offered him by Honest Sam. The trouble is that when he finally completes the deal with Honest Sam he does not get the original "appraisal" price.)

"The noncommittal customer." LEVEL WITH HIM! Tell him you've shot your wad and that if he'll tell you WHAT'S WRONG WITH THE DEAL you'll beat your brains out to get it from the house. When the chips are down . . . DON'T FORGET TO SAY WHY.

(This last sentence means that when the salesman comes back shaking his head sadly and saying the boss won't let him make that deal—"but we're only $200 apart"—he ought to have plausible reasons, such as: "We'll have to do at least $200 worth of body work on your old car to make it salable.")

"I'm shopping." Sit them down and explain to them how the car business has changed since they last traded for a new one. Explain that ALL dealers are working on practically an identical margin for the new car, and picking up their profit on the used one. Tell them that no matter how many miles they travel or how many dealers they shop, the deals will vary less than $15. Then sell the house and the man and the fact that your new car is $90 better than any new car in the area because of the way your dealership falls over backwards on predelivery expense and warranty services.

Ringer also has some suggestions for "cold spearing" customers on the street. One such spiel begins this way:

Pardon me, madam, I hate like everything to come up to you cold turkey like this, but I sell used cars at——— Motors, and we've been looking high and low for a car exactly like yours. If you can figure a way to sell me this car now, I can give you so much gold for it that you can afford to take your groceries and kids home on your back. . . .

A similar patter has been developed for telephone sales:

"Good evening, Mrs. Jones, this is Bates of———Motors calling. Did you call me?"
Not me, I didn't call anybody.
"Well, I'll be darned. I work in a team with another salesman here and we sell Fords and used cars. I thought perhaps you had been talking to him and that he wanted me to follow the deal up. . . .
Nope. 'Fraid not, I ain't interested in no new car.
"Funny thing how I got your number. What kind of a car do you drive?"
A '46 Ford.
"Oh! Oh! THAT'S why I was supposed to call you. We've been looking high and low for a sharp '46 Ford and my partner must have gotten your name, etc. . . ."

In thirty-seven cases out of a hundred, says the astute Mr. Ringer of Hollywood, such a call produces "action."

If these techniques do not appeal to the sense of larceny in every man, they at least appeal to his avarice. The success of the spurious "contests," now deeply ingrained in the standard direct-sales techniques of dozens of companies all over the continent, testifies to this principle. As in Alice's caucus race, everybody who takes part in such contests is a winner, so all must have prizes. These prizes are usually known as "consolation" prizes, but they provide little real consolation to those who find that they end up paying for them.

One of the most preposterous of these contests was held by a short-lived firm called Z-All Home and Farm Accessories, which managed to sell thousands of dollars worth of cheap cookware, vacuum cleaners, dishes, and other merchandise in rural Canada. The technique here was to mail out to farm areas a postal reply card containing a questionnaire regarding electrical equipment in the home and offering $10,-000 worth of free gifts in a lucky draw.

Thousands who sent in their cards for the draw were later visited by salesmen who told them that theirs was one of three lucky names picked in that county to receive $1,000 worth of merchandise for "advertising purposes." First, however, there was another little contest. The respondents had to answer three simple questions correctly: *What is the longest river in Canada? What is the Queen City? What province is Ottawa situated in?* In spite of the simplicity of these questions, which any grade-5 schoolchild in the province of Ontario is equipped to answer, the salesmen were invariably able to demonstrate that the respondents had in some way got one answer wrong.

Still, this entitled them to a consolation prize. They would be given all the merchandise—$1,000 worth—for a mere $299. Actually, the salesmen pointed out, these were free since all the respondents had to do was to supply the names of ten newly married couples in the neighborhood and they would receive $250. (The remaining $49 was for "packaging and handling.") And, if the merchandise didn't suit them, why, the company would send along a catalogue of items for which they could exchange it if they wanted. But they were told they must pay the $250 at once; the offer would not be repeated.

A surprising number of farm families succumbed—and soon found themselves loaded down with cheap merchandise which they didn't want. Needless to say, the catalogues were not forthcoming. As for those newly married couples, it developed that each of them must actually buy a like quantity of merchandise from the company before the promised bonus would be paid to the original respondents.

The contest gimmick is a favorite door-opening device for companies pushing vacuum cleaners, floor polishers, cookware, and sewing machines. A Mr. L. Hartney, of 103 Parkside Drive, Toronto, was one such winner in 1959. This is the letter that was mailed to Mr. Hartney:

> Congratulations! You have been awarded a Consolation Prize by our Board of Judges. Enclosed you will find a $25.00 consolation certificate which can be deducted from the price of any of the items illustrated. For your convenience we have enclosed a card which entitles you to a free home demonstration.

In this case, it was no contest. Mr. Hartney had been dead for seven years.

Atlas Sewing Centres actually named "winners" of the first and second prizes on its mailing piece, and I was curious enough to check into one of these, since he appeared to be a man of the cloth. The Reverend J. J. O'Leary, of Sault Ste. Marie, Ontario, was listed as a first-prize winner in one Atlas contest; but when Father O'Leary was reached by phone he explained that he had not entered any contest. The firm had tried to give him a free vacuum cleaner and he had returned it immediately. That did not stop them from using his name. But later on, this company and a similar firm, Super Master Appliances (which sent out almost identical letters), dropped the names of first- and second-prize "winners."

The technique continues to be successful in spite of the many ironies that these mass mailings produce. Inconsistencies do not bother the sales managers any more than public

exposure does, since they have learned that a certain percentage of the public will always reply once it has been
named a "winner." It does not matter that the contest is not
specified. It does not matter that the winners didn't enter the
contest—and know it. It does not matter that these letters
are shamelessly mimeographed forms. They have won $25
somehow, somewhere, for something; why question it? One
gets the feeling that it might be possible to walk down the
street passing out envelopes to people, pumping their hands
in congratulation, and crying: "You've won! You've won!"
without having any of them ask: *Won what?* People expect
to win something these days; it has become part of Our Way
of Life. Only occasionally do they question the motives of
the contest manager when the prize seems a little outlandish.
There was, of course, the case of Mary Axford, in Toronto,
who was telephoned on innumerable occasions by the Patricia Stevens Finishing School and given the news that she
had been chosen the city's ideal debutante. The school offered to give her a free analysis in order to improve her
speech, her beauty, her figure, and her deportment. The
lucky girl tried to make it clear that she did not want to be
the ideal debutante, but Patricia Stevens kept calling and
doing her best to thrust the award upon her. Mary Axford
never did succeed in getting across the point that at the age
of eighty-one she felt a little old for such frivolities.

In some cases, there actually is a contest of sorts. Elna
Sewing Centres (Canada) Ltd., for example, sponsored an
"easy word game," which it sent through the mails. A kinder-
garten child would have had difficulty failing this test of wit,
but thousands who were told they had won acted as if their
ship had come in. The contest listed 10 first prizes of $100,
20 second prizes of $50, and 40 third prizes of $25—well, not
money actually—gift certificates. A man I know who worked
for this firm told me that as fast as the contest entries poured

into the Elna office, $50 certificates were mailed out—for everyone. It was his job at one point to call upon the lucky winners, break the news of their good fortune, and sell them a sewing machine. The basic price at the time was $299, and this was the price that both the lucky winners and the regular customers invariably paid. But the lucky winners were told that the retail price was $349 and that they could have the machine for $299 plus their certificate. My man told me a little sadly that many of them burst into tears of joy when the news of their fabulous winnings was broken to them.

The technique of some of these companies—Super Master Appliances was one—is to depict, on the letter to the lucky winners, the actual merchandise that they can buy at bargain rates by using their gift certificates. There is a sewing machine shown at $49.95 (or a mere $24.95, with the gift certificate); a floor polisher at $44.50; and a vacuum cleaner, with "all attachments necessary for a thorough job of housecleaning," at a mere $39.50. With the gift certificate, of course, this vacuum would sell for the impossibly low sum of $14.50. I have yet to meet anyone who was actually able to buy one. The technique is to sell a much more expensive product.

6

The power of suggestion is an important factor in the big sell. Part of the truth is often more effective than all of it, and a good deal of direct selling seems to depend as much on what is left out as on what is included. This is also a form of deception, but a subtle one. The sensitive salesman can soothe his conscience by telling himself that he hasn't been a party to a single lie.

Here, for instance, is the main portion of the official sales pitch of the Combined Insurance Company of America for its "Little Giant" policy. It contains no untruths or even exaggerations, and the reader, studying it carefully, may easily come to the conclusion that the "Little Giant" policy is a pretty good buy. (I have again included, in bracketed italics, the company's instructions to its salesmen.)

I believe this will interest you ALSO! For ONLY 12 cents a week we are giving a special $2,000 Accident Policy. We have a TREMENDOUS number of people carrying our policy. By the way, perhaps you know (*show lots of names—each member of the family separately, including children*).

As I was saying, for ONLY 12 cents a week, should you lose your LIFE! SIGHT! LIMBS! or anything as shown here, we pay $2,000 each six months, $50 more until it reaches $2,500. In case you are hurt as shown here, we pay one of the *highest* weekly incomes *ever* paid in proportion to the premium. *Fifteen dollars a week* beginning with the *very first day* and for a period of 15 weeks. *Just* think of it! For ONLY 12 cents a week! Or, if you wish to, you can do as most people do—and for ONLY 24 cents a week take the full unit. That is two policies and you receive $4,000 increasing to $5,000 and a wonderful weekly income of $30 a week or in other words *One Hundred and Thirty Dollars a Month.* . . .

We pay if you are hurt. (*Continue to smile*) We even pay you if your feelings are hurt. How's that? Ha! Ha! Ha! Ha!

Seriously, we don't do that, but should you take a trip to Winnipeg, Calgary, Vancouver, Montreal, a vacation to the States or elsewhere, we cover you as shown here on the train and other public conveyance, *of course.* You may or may not have flown in an airplane but if you ever *do* we cover you as a fare-paying passenger on a regular scheduled flight to *any* part of the world. *Just* think of it!

(*Don't hesitate too long here*) Or you may lose your life as shown here...... Five hundred dollars on one! One thousand dollars on the full unit!—BY BEING STRUCK! KNOCKED DOWN OR RUN OVER!—BY ANY MOVING VEHICLE! DRIVING! OR RIDING! IN ANY AUTOMOBILE, BUS, TROLLEY, TAXICAB OR TRUCK! AT THE HANDS OF ANY BURGLAR, HIGH-WAYMAN OR ROBBER! DROWNING! In case of fire or suffo-cation by smoke, we cover you right here in your place of business.....at home.....or in *Any* BURNING BUILD-ING!

Here's something you will find in *very* few policies in Canada today. If any of these accidents require: MEDICAL OR SURGICAL TREATMENT AT THE PLACE OF ACCIDENT: AM-BULANCE SERVICE TO OR FROM A HOSPITAL: ANY SERVICES OF A PHYSICIAN, CHIROPRACTOR OR OSTEOPATH AT A HOSPITAL. ..... For every day such services are necessary we pay *you* in cash $4 a day to a total of $56.....*plus* $15 a week loss of time on the one.....or we pay *you* in cash $8 a day to a total of $112, *plus* $30 a week loss of time on the full unit......

Anyone hearing this line of patter may be tempted to ask: *How can they offer so much for a mere 12 cents a week?* The fact is that, although some hundreds of thousands of people have bought such policies, they are being offered very little, as a careful look at the actual policy makes clear.

In the first place, for your beneficiary to collect the $2,000, you must be killed. And you must be killed while riding as a fare-paying passenger on the regular run of a railway, sub-way car, streetcar, or passenger boat, or in an elevator or in a regularly scheduled airplane. On no other form of death will the $2,000 be paid.

If you're not killed outright, you cannot collect a cent for the accident unless you actually lose a hand, a foot, or an eye. The payments here range from $200 for the loss of one eye to $2,000 for the loss of *both* eyes, *both* hands, or *both* feet.

There is a lesser sum of $500 payable if you are killed in one of several very specific ways:

If you are struck by a moving vehicle on a public highway; if you are killed while riding in or driving an automobile, bus, trolley, taxi, or truck; if you are killed while being robbed; if you drown; or if you are inside a burning building in which you are specifically burned or have suffocated from smoke, your beneficiary would collect. But if you run into a burning building to save somebody and are killed, your beneficiary cannot collect.

The weekly indemnity of $15 and the medical benefits of $56 apply to these specific accidents *only*—nothing else.

Recently, a man who held one of these policies was badly injured when his kitchen stove exploded. He tried to claim under the fire clause, but the company pointed out that the building must be burning. It didn't burn—only the stove.

Recently, a man with one of these policies was seriously injured when his motorcycle struck the back of a truck. He could not collect a cent because motorcycles aren't covered. Trucks are, but you must be struck by a moving truck: this one wasn't moving.

Recently, a man with one of these policies was killed when his car skidded in a gas station and smashed up. His beneficiary could not collect since the policy specifically points out that such accidents must occur on a public highway.

The company can charge such a low premium—it comes to $3 every six months—because the chances that these accidents will happen to many people are comparatively slight. That's why it does not cost much to have a double-indemnity clause added to your life insurance. It is also useful to note that the company can cancel the policy at the end of any six-months period without giving the policyholder any reason.

It can also use it as a springboard to sell a much costlier policy at the end of the six-months period.

The sales pitch is a very clever one. It contrives to suggest at the outset that the policy covers all accidents. It also contrives to suggest that it covers many injuries. ("Should you lose your life, sight, limbs, or *anything as shown here,* we pay $2,000.") The reference to vehicles is only brought in later and in such a way that it seems to be an extra—not a specifically confining clause. The idea that two policies will pay double is also subtly introduced. They will: *if*—and only if—two people are killed or injured.

Yet there are no out-and-out lies told here. The cheery salesman asks if he may write out the policy. If he follows instructions, he "hesitates four or five seconds while using the McCabe nod"—a hypnotic bobbing of the head, which has been compared to a conjurer forcing a card on a sucker. The mesmerized prospect signs. If he reads the policy carefully, it will tell him exactly what he has bought—and what he hasn't; but the chances are he will not read it until it's too late.

A similar technique is often used by the gaudier mail-order companies to describe their products. This seems to apply especially to certain mail-order nursery firms. The strategy here is to pretend that the plant, shrub, or flower is "new" and then to use a dazzling variety of descriptive phrases which, while not strictly untruths, are open to a variety of interpretations. In the spring of 1960, for instance, thousands of householders in eastern Canada and the United States were bombarded with four-color brochures and huge newspaper ads singing the praises of a supposedly new tree called the Ailanthus. The descriptive material about this tree was a masterpiece of the copywriter's art, but some of the claims made for the tree were open to several interpretations.

Now! The most amazing garden offer in the past fifty years!

The word "now" and the word "amazing" (the ubiquitous clichés of the ad world) suggest that the tree is a new one. Actually it has been known for decades. It is the same Tree That Grew in Brooklyn in the Betty Smith novel.

Grows roof high in just one single season.

Under perfect conditions of soil and water, if the roof is on a small toolshed, perhaps. One sample tree, planted in Toronto the previous spring, had attained the tremendous height of three feet eleven inches by the following fall.

A fantastic super-growing variety that in just one single season grows higher than even a full-grown maple tree.

The ad did not explain what kind of a maple tree it was referring to. A red maple reaches a full height of 120 feet; the Ailanthus will grow to 60 feet, but not in a single season. There are Japanese dwarf maples, however, which never grow as high as a man, and in later advertising this phrase was amended to "Japanese red maple."

For a truly dramatic effect it lavishes its branches with dazzling bouquets of beautiful flowers . . . like a magnificent flower garden growing in the sky.

What the ad did not say was that the flowers, if numerous, are small and inconspicuous—because they are green.

A few minutes to plant and your garden is turned into a shaded summer paradise.

Like everything else, the Ailanthus casts a shadow, but because of its rank and open growth the shadow is one of the sparsest cast by any tree. It takes exactly the same time to plant, of course, as any other tree.

One of the most amazing shade trees ever introduced to the people of North America . . . the Pride of Great Britain.

This again contrived to suggest that the tree was a new import. It was not. What the ad did not mention was that the Ailanthus is also known in the trade as "Stinkweed" because the flowers of the female tree and the entire male tree have a noxious and disagreeable odor. Pollen from the flowers often troubles people with allergies.

. . . *casting its cooling shade through the New York Botanical Gardens.* . . .

Any botanical garden might be expected to have samples of most trees, including the Ailanthus. The ad did not say, of course, that it was banned entirely from the streets of Indianapolis.

Never in your life have you seen a tree multiply in value, multiply in growth, like this tower-tall flowering tree.

The Ailanthus certainly multiplies. It is a messy tree which drops its seeds, and these, plus suckers from the roots, keep it producing young saplings and shoots faster than a busy gardener can pull them out. It takes root not only in the lawn but also in cracks in sewer pipes and sidewalks. Note the repeated use here of the word "flowering tree"; all trees, of course, have flowers of a sort.

Now the price of these super-growing shade trees on this no-risk trial offer is not the $15 or $20 apiece that you might expect to pay for a shade tree . . . but a mere $3.98.

You might expect to pay $15 or $20 for one of the rarer trees in the larger sizes, but one prominent nurseryman told me that if he wanted to carry the Ailanthus (which he did not) he could get it for five cents apiece wholesale.

Though the Ailanthus was said to be "praised by garden editors the world over," it was also marked "not recommended" by the New Jersey Federation of Shade Tree Commissions, called a "trash tree or worse" by Henry Chase, a prominent nurseryman in Alabama, and labeled "a nuisance and an undesirable weed" by Norman Scott, one of Canada's best-known nurserymen.

The Ailanthus promotion reminded me of the time when, as a novice gardener, I read with awe similar advertisements for an amazing new Wonder Flower from the wilds of Tibet, guaranteed to produce "armfuls of dazzling bloom." I sent in my $3.98 and in return received six tiny chrysanthemum shoots, worth about fifty cents.

Musing this over, I decided to try the experiment of writing mail-order type advertisements for five well-known weeds. Every word of the copy that follows is true. The pictures are taken from F. Schuyler Matthews' *Field Book of American Wild Flowers*.

NOW! From Europe comes the amazing GOLDEN CROWN . . . . . a flower you simply can't be without!

Yes, we positively guarantee that no more prolific plant exists. Once in your garden it's yours forever. Deep-rooted and hardy, it will sustain the worst frosts or the hottest spells of a rainless summer.

Easy to grow . . . requires little cultivation . . . resists weeds. IT WILL EVEN GROW IN TURF!

Imagine armfuls of brilliant yellow flowers suffusing your home with the aura of pure gold! Think of it—for a small initial investment this year you can have *bushels of golden bloom* in just one, two, or three seasons, because GOLDEN CROWN multiplies by itself! No need to buy expensive replacements. . . . . . Thanks to this amazing zinnia-like plant, you can have *fields of flowers for only a few cents*.

Yes, that's right. . . . . imagine a sheet of solid yellow brightening your driveway next May. You'll be the envy of the neighbors if you buy GOLDEN CROWN. . . . .

Special offer for one week: 6 plants. . . . . . ONLY $5.62

The INCREDIBLE SNOWSTORM PLANT! *Now at Bargain Rates!*
You won't want to be without this fantastic novelty—a
delight for children and adults
and an asset to any garden
. . . . known in ancient Greece,
where it was called *asclepias,*
the SNOWSTORM PLANT is now
available here in limited quantities. . . . One of the few
flowering perennials that actually imitates *an actual snowstorm.*

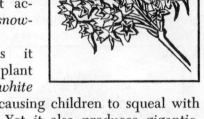

Yes, unbelievable as it
sounds, this Snowstorm plant
sends off *blizzards of white
bloom,* causing children to squeal with
delight. Yet it also produces gigantic,
lilac-colored flowers—each one a slightly
different hue.

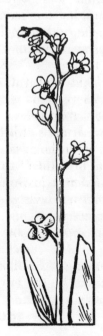

*No other plant like it! Don't dissap-
point your children! Be the first in your
neighborhood to own and grow the
plant that everybody's talking about!* 6
plants. . . . . ONLY $3.95

*Who Else Wants a Garden of Pale Green
and Glittering Pink?*
That's what you'll have when you
plant PINK MAGIC, the incredible new
plant imported from the wilds of con-
tinental Asia. A close relative of the for-
get-me-not, PINK MAGIC actually grows
much taller, while its delicate flowers
are pure magenta pink. The Chinese
have known about this plant for years.

Now it can be yours, too, for a fraction of the original cost, absolutely guaranteed against frost, drought, or garden pests. *Yes, that's right! We guarantee that* PINK MAGIC *cannot be killed by normal garden conditions, that it can even grow in subsoil, even in thick weeds.*

Imagine owning a flower you don't have to weed and that seeds itself year after year without further expense or trouble to you. *And it blooms all summer* . . . . . .

But that's not all: Pink Magic's soft gray-green foliage will delight you. The unique velvet leaves provide a background that will make you the envy of the neighborhood. Order your PINK MAGIC *plants while they last.*

8 plants. . . . . ONLY $4.23

AT LAST! A perennial flower that grows MAN SIZE in just two months. . . .

Yes, we know it's hard to believe, but when you get your amazing new SKYSCRAPER PLANT you'll discover that *miracles can happen!*

Think of it! A flower that can grow as high as six feet in a single summer and produce masses of lemon-yellow bloom on spikes *as long as three feet! And these giant spikes of flowers last —not just for days—but for weeks!*

Can you imagine the oohs! and aahs! of your friends when they see one of these luxurious giant Skyscraper Plants lofting above your home? And can you imagine the envy with which they'll greet a vase topped by one of these incredible mammoth flowers?

Easy to grow, these luxurious Mediterranean plants come absolutely guaranteed to withstand the Canadian winter. But act quickly to avoid disappointment!

2 plants. . . . . .ONLY $5.75

Now from the mountain fastness of Eurasia comes a flower as delicate as a lace doily!

ABSOLUTELY UNIQUE, these enormous flowers seem to have been crocheted by hand by a master seamstress! Often half a foot across, these gigantic blooms will thrill you both in the garden and in the home because *there is no other flower in the world quite like them!*

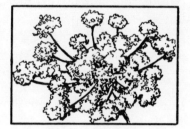

Born on sturdy stalks, growing as high as a school-age child, these delicately fashioned blooms last and last and last. . . . . .

Just imagine your perennial border in July and August dominated by these *unbelievable saucer-sized blossoms* which will come back, year after year, requiring little or no care to make your home a showplace. *From the steppes of Central Russia to you for* ONLY $1.98

The reader has perhaps guessed the names of some of these plants. They are, in order, the common dandelion, the milkweed, the common bur (or hound's-tongue), the great mullein, and the Queen Anne's lace (or wild carrot). Three are considered so noxious that in my neighborhood it is a crime for any farmer to allow them to grow uncut after July 1.

I published the results of this experiment in my column in ⋅ the Toronto *Star,* being careful to explain that these were really weeds. At the end of the column, I named them all. This did not stop one couple from mailing me a check for $3.95 for six Incredible Snowstorm Plants. I returned the check, explaining what the column was all about and pointing out that I had tried to make this clear. I received, in reply, a torrent of abuse for my fakery, together with a canceled subscription and the promise that they and their friends, who were also planning to buy the Incredible Snowstorm Plants, would never again believe another word I wrote. Hell hath no fury like a mooch unmasked.

2

The Anatomy of the Classic Con

Jacob Thurston[1] did not know he was an Egg. Even after he had lost the $3,300, he did not know he was an Egg. But when he sat down in the Canadian National Station in Edmonton, Alberta, he was spotted immediately as an Egg and a very special kind of Egg at that—not a Bite Egg or a Match Egg or a Payoff Egg, but a Duke Egg.

The signs were all there if you could read them, and the thin-faced Steer man, sauntering casually about the lobby, read them at once. It was not only the tousled hair, the shrewd, small eyes, and the big, freckled hands; there was also an aura that said that Thurston was not above making a fast

[1] All the names have been changed in this chapter.

55

dollar, that he fancied himself a shrewd man in a deal, that he felt like a fish out of water in Edmonton, and that he did not have too much experience with the world.

The thin-faced man sat down beside Jacob Thurston, asked him for a match, and began a genial, casual conversation. It was not long before Thurston volunteered the information that he was from the little town of Stony Plain.

"Stony Plain?" asked the thin-faced man in surprise. "Did you say Stony Plain?" Thurston nodded.

"Now *there's* a coincidence!" said the thin-faced man. "How long have you lived there?" Thurston told him proudly that he was born and raised in Stony Plain. The thin-faced man caught him by the arm.

"Look," he said earnestly, "before I say anything more I would like you to give me your word of honor that you will never expose anything I'm going to tell you." Thurston nodded and leaned forward with interest.

"My name is Blake," said the thin-faced man. "I'm from back East, but the odd thing is that I'm on my way down to Stony Plain. I'm looking for a piece of property in that area. I was in town on other business, but I have to attend to this matter for my two brothers. Now, look: I don't want any of this to come to the attention of real-estate agents. I don't want any sharp-shooters in the know. They'll put a bill of goods over on you if they can and, as I'm not familiar at all with this territory, I could easily be sold a lemon. Now you know the area and you know the farms. Do you know of any that are actually for sale? There could be a nice piece of change in it for you if you're willing to keep your mouth shut."

"I think so," said Thurston. "Will Osborne would sell if he got a decent offer." And, as they began to discuss Will Osborne's farm, the man who called himself Blake could see the wheels turning in the other's head and he knew from long observation of his fellows that Will Osborne's farm was a lemon and the Egg was planning to make a good thing out of it.

"Look," he said. "What time does your train go out? Six? Well, you've got three hours to kill. I was just sitting here waiting. I don't know the city at all. Why don't we go over somewhere and have a bottle of beer together?" Jacob Thurston, mentally calculating the cut of the profit he would get from Will Osborne as well as from the gullible stranger, cheerfully agreed.

When Thurston suggested a second bottle of beer, Blake, the Steer man, knew that he was caught. He was looking quietly around for the Takeoff man, whose name that day was to be Billy Moore. He appeared, almost on cue, and seeing the Steer man, burst into a whoop of surprise:

"For God's sake. You're Jack Blake!"

"Billy Moore! Where on earth did you spring from?"

"Why, I been in town three months."

"Aren't you doing any work these days, Billy? Doesn't your old man get sick of feeding you money all the time?"

"He might get sick of it, but he's still giving it to me. He better not stop!"

The conversation continued, the Takeoff man still standing and the Steer man acting toward him with just a slight suggestion of disdain.

"Oh, come on—you better sit down and have a beer with us. God Almighty, you're blocking the aisle where you are," the Steer man finally said, and as he did so, he turned to Thurston and gave a slight shrug.

After some conversation, the Takeoff man excused himself and went to the men's room.

"I've known him all my life," Blake explained to Thurston. "He's all right, but he's a showoff. His father's money buys him out of everything. Actually he's never done a tap of real

57

work. He isn't like you. He's mooched off his father all his life. I don't know how he stands it. Personally, *I've* earned every dime I've ever got."

Thurston was warming to Blake. He saw that they had a good deal in common, including their disdain of Billy Moore, the prodigal son.

When Moore returned, he suggested they go up to his room, but Blake demurred. Moore said he had a letter from his sister, who had been asking about Blake. Blake allowed himself to be persuaded, and the three adjourned to Moore's hotel. There was some light conversation and a few jokes with a slight suggestion of sex to them. Blake showed a couple of tricks with matches. ("Can you spell Child's Restaurant with five matches? No? Here's how," and he formed the letters TIT.)

"Wait a minute, I got another one," he said. "Hey, Moore, have you got a pack of cards about?"

"Oh, I guess I've got a deck somewhere," Moore said. He found them, and Blake proceeded to show a few simple card tricks.

"Let's have a hand of rummy," Moore suggested, but Blake shook his head. "I can't stand that game," he said. "Fact is, I'm not much of a card player at all. I've never really bothered with cards in my life."

"Oh, come on," said Moore. "You must know some kind of a game to pass an hour. How about Spit-in-the-Ocean?"

"The only game I've ever played is English High Pair, and I'm no good at that," said Blake. He explained that in this card game a high pair usually won since straights and flushes had no value. After some further prodding by Moore, he agreed to play a hand or two, and it was decided that all bets would be a nickel, with raises limited to the size of the pot. It would serve to while away the time before the train left, said Blake, and the winner would have to buy the beer.

It sounded innocent enough. Thurston, the Egg, won the first pot—about eight dollars—and with it the deal. He pushed the pack over to Moore, on his right, who casually cut the cards. In doing so, Moore placed a "cap" of one dozen carefully arranged cards on the top of the pack. It was his habit to carry such a cap in his pocket for just such a purpose and to transfer it to his inner palm whenever a game began. For it was no simple card game these three were now engaged in; the game is known in the argot of the con fraternity as the Duke (so called because the Takeoff man's job at this point is to get his "dukes" on the deck). It can be a very expensive pastime. In Vancouver, in 1929, an Egg was relieved of $50,000 playing the game that Jacob Thurston played.

Thurston dealt one card down and one card face up, and each player discovered he had a pair. Blake had deuces; Moore had jacks; and Thurston, to his elation, found himself with aces.

"Hey, you're pretty lucky!" his friend Blake told him. "You sure know what you're doing. Look, if you want to waive the size of the pot, that's okay by me. We'll make the winner buy a couple of bottles of whiskey for the train."

Thurston eagerly agreed and bet a quarter. Blake called the bet and raised it half a dollar. Moore saw that bet and raised it two dollars, and the pot began to build.

"Hold on a minute," said Blake. "This is too steep for me. All I got is two deuces. You guys have me beat." He turned over his cards, pulled back his chair, and went over behind Thurston. From then on, he controlled Thurston's play as surely as a hypnotist controls his subject.

A whispered side conversation went on for the rest of the game between the Egg and his new friend, who appeared to have joined forces with him against the overly confident Moore. ("Look," Blake would say to Thurston, "this guy deserves a lesson. He thinks money will take him anywhere. Just because I know him don't hesitate to soak it to him. . . . Don't worry; that guy can afford to lose and, if you ask me, it's time he lost at something.")

Before the third card was played, Thurston and Moore, through raises and counter-raises, had put $50 in the pot.

The third card did not improve Moore's hand. Thurston, however, drew a king, and this increased his sense of elation. He found himself tossing $50 into the pot and then, when Moore raised, $200. By the time the fourth card was drawn, the pot had grown to several hundred dollars.

On the fourth card Thurston drew a second king, and the betting increased as the two men called and raised back and forth.

Thurston ran out of cash and asked if a check would be acceptable. Moore agreed, since he, too, was out of cash and wanted to use checks, and the betting continued. Moore now appeared to be less cocky and more and more nervous. Finally he announced that as far as he was concerned the betting was over. He turned to Blake.

"You understand this game a lot better than I do," he said. "As far as I can see, he has me beat, and I'm sorry I got into it at all. What I want to know is this—is there anything at all that could beat two high pair? He's got two there. He must have. Is there anything that can beat them, or am I wasting my time? Should I give him the pot right now?"

"You might as well," said Blake, and then added casually: "Well, theoretically I suppose you could win with three of a kind, but that's hopeless—it's a mathematical rarity."

"Well," said Moore, "what do you say we let the fifth card decide it?" This was agreeable to Thurston, who discovered that, in the space of a few minutes, he had put $3,300 in cash and checks into the pot.

Before the fifth card was dealt, however, Blake insisted on

protecting Thurston's interests: Moore would simply have to produce cash for the checks he had written. After all, Blake pointed out, Thurston was from out of town; he didn't know Moore; and he might not see him again when the game was done; it was only fair, then, that he take his winnings in cash. Blake insinuated that Moore was just the type of man to stop the checks before Thurston could get them cashed. He turned to get Thurston's assent, and the farmer agreed enthusiastically. Of course, he said, he was prepared to get cash for his checks, too, as a token of good faith.[2]

A small ceremony followed. Each hand was sealed separately with Scotch tape. The pack itself was sealed. The cards, together with the money and the checks, were placed in an envelope. The envelope was sealed, with the signatures of all three participants scrawled across the flap to prevent anyone's tampering with it.

The train was forgotten. Thurston and his new friend hired a taxi and drove the twenty miles to Stony Plain, where the farmer got his cash. Then they returned to the hotel room, where Moore was awaiting them.

The envelope was unsealed and the last card dealt. Moore drew a jack face up. Thurston's hand did not improve.

When the cards were turned over, it was quickly revealed that Moore's three jacks beat Thurston's two pairs.

[2] Thus the confidence game known as the Duke was transformed into a variation known as the Payoff Duke. In the simpler version nobody goes for money. The Steer man, who always has a set of dummy checks in his pocket, insists that the friendly little game has gone too far, that the checks ought to be removed from the pot and the game confined to cash betting alone. He then pretends to tear up and burn the checks in front of the Egg, but, in fact, does nothing of the kind. When the game is ended, the Egg is kept occupied while the Takeoff man cashes the real checks. In this instance, however, the Steer man sensed that Thurston would be quite willing to go back to Stony Plain for the money. Since it is becoming increasingly difficult to cozen banks into cashing checks of this size without inquiry, the alternative plan was better.

"My God!" said Blake to Moore in surprise. "Do you mean to tell me you went all that way with a pair of jacks? How lucky can you get on the last card?"

"I thought he was bluffing there at first," said Moore, raking in the cash. "I thought he was trying to buy the pot. Then I got cold feet, but now I'm glad I stayed."

For the first moment or two, Thurston's reaction was stunned silence. Then he broke out in a rage—not at Blake or Moore but at himself. He slammed his fist so heavily on the table he all but cracked it.

"It's my own fault!" he cried out.

"My own fault! I should have known better."

He wheeled around and gave Blake a momentarily hostile look.

"Don't blame me," said Blake. "I told you three or four times that you shouldn't bluff, but you wouldn't pay any attention."

"You did?" asked Thurston in bewilderment.

"You didn't even hear me, I guess, in the excitement of the game," said Blake. "But now look. The last thing that you and I want to do is quarrel. I'm partly responsible for this— at least fifty per cent. If you'd bet your cards properly, you wouldn't be in that last round, but never mind. It isn't much money—half of $3,300—and I'm going to make it good. I'll get on the phone and get it. You'll get twice that, anyway, when our deal is completed; I can promise you that. I won't deal with anybody else but you. I told you that at the beginning and that's the way it's going to be."

He went to the phone, made a call, and then returned.

"I'm having the money sent right away," he said. "Now, meantime, they want more details on this Stony Plain property."

And so Thurston, still somewhat stunned but ever hopeful, returned to Stony Plain with Blake, who made a great show of being interested in the Will Osborne property. Off he went to Edmonton, promising to return immediately with Thurston's cash and close the deal. But he did not return, then or ever, and the bewildered Thurston still waits and wonders how he could have lost $3,300 on a single hand of cards in the space of less than an hour while waiting for a train.

2

Any student of the classic confidence games must be struck by the several parallels they present with some modern big-sell techniques. The confidence man sells nothing but himself, of course, while the salesman peddles more tangible merchandise; but the psychological techniques each employs are remarkably similar.

The classic con games preceded the big sell and have been polished and perfected over three quarters of a century, ever since the days in Creede, Colorado, when Jefferson Randolph Smith earned his nickname of "Soapy" by convincing the customers there was a bank note concealed beneath every wrapper of shaving soap.

The dialogue of the con games is memorized almost to the exact phrase, so that a good Steer man or Spiel man or Tail man can walk into any city in the world, make contact with others of his craft, and begin to play the classic Duke, Match, Bite, Payoff, or Rag. Except for the Bite, all these games are based on a shrewd observation of human nature: that there is a little bit of larceny in most of us. Having gained the confidence of the Egg, the Steer man must then convince him that he can make a large sum of money, usually at somebody else's expense.

The Egg, then, has three qualities. He is, first of all, a man who wants to be in on a sure thing. He is, second, a person who can be manipulated through the warmth of personal relationship and through subtle methods of flattery. He is, third, a man who is unsure of himself. In the classic con games, the Egg is always a traveler in a strange city. But in the legal games of the big sell, the Egg is simply someone seeking guidance: a newcomer from a foreign land, often enough; or a gullible housewife with no one to talk to; or a young spinster trying to achieve self-assurance through dancing lessons.

I have an acquaintance who happens to be one of the best con men on the continent. He is a master psychologist, a consummate actor, and a highly educated expert in the ways of the world. He can slide easily into half a dozen dialects, and I know of no stage performer who can touch him. He not only has the accents down pat, but he has also studied speech patterns and idioms so he can take on the role of a Polish immigrant and suddenly *look* Polish. I once asked him to try to explain the psychology by which a stranger in a railway station can, in a few minutes, exert such a hold over another man that that man will trust him with his life savings. Here is the way it went onto the tape recorder:

"You never attempt to con a man in his own town. That is why you choose people who are traveling. In the first place, the Egg's mind is free; you must be able to capture his full attention to beat him. You see, he isn't sure of himself and he's glad to talk to someone when he's alone and traveling.

"He's a different man altogether when he's not at home. At home he feels secure. No one can tell him anything that he doesn't have a preconceived idea about. At home he'd argue with you. Now, when he's being steered you can tell him almost anything because he's on a trip and he's seen things he didn't know existed before. This shakes him. He's not so sure of the things he once thought he knew. There's doubt in his mind. Maybe there are other things he doesn't know about. Maybe the ideas and opinions he's held could be revised.

"A man away from home is like a fish out of water. If you're able to understand his psychology and think a step or two ahead of him, then you're filling a void that he needs filled. He's been among people all his life that he knows well. Now, suddenly, he's alone and out of his element.

"So a con man comes along who understands exactly how he feels. He knows the man is lonely and yet slightly suspicious. He knows he's slightly off balance psychologically. The con man reads all this in a few seconds. With a single look he can tell if the Egg is a Duke man or a Bite man or a Match man.

"Before the Egg realizes it he is saying to himself: 'Well, I know this stranger is all right.'

"Your Egg has to be a believer. Even a sophisticated man can be a believer. In this case he believes in *you*. Why he should place his confidence in a stranger is very difficult to explain. But what he does is to project an image of himself which is accepted and reflected by the con man. When that happens, the Egg would do anything in the world rather than part from you.

"It's rather like a man in love. He projects an image of himself to the girl. She flatters him and raves about him so he begins to believe that the image is *really* himself. He'd do anything on earth rather than destroy that image of himself. That's why, when some romances break up, the people involved have difficulty in adjusting. When the girl finally refuses her man, the image is shattered and he can't put it back together again—and so his personality is shattered.

"Well, the Egg is the same way and I've seen them shat-

65

tered just as badly. The confidence man is like a seducer. The hold he has over the Egg isn't sexual of course, but the parallel is there. You let the Egg see, through you, the flattering image he wants to project of himself. When he sees you are accepting that image, he will do absolutely anything you ask of him."

In salesmanship it is also the image that counts—and it matters little that the image is often phony.

Con games are not played for peanuts. Even in a simple game like the Match, which resembles the Duke but revolves around coin-tossing on the street, an Egg can lose $1,000 in the space of a few minutes. Yet Eggs seldom squawk to the police, partly because they are ashamed and embarrassed and partly because no good con game ever ends when the Egg parts with his money. An elaborate mechanism has been worked out to ensure that the Egg is never alone in the hours or the days that follow; he is still under the influence of the Steer man, whose job is first to confuse him and then to convince him that he has been involved in a shady enterprise which can never be revealed.

The one major con game that does not play on the larceny of the Egg is the Bite, in which a good operator can single-handedly pick up one hundred dollars from a likely looking Egg in about seven minutes. The Bite is based entirely on trust.

"You got to size up your man," an expert in the game once told me. "Some are Match Eggs and some are Duke Eggs. A Bite Egg is a different kind of Egg. It's hard to put into words, but it is chiefly character, kindliness of expression, and general demeanor."

In the Bite, the only equipment needed is a ten-cent newspaper. The game, like most confidence games, is traditionally played at the railway station (and today, though less frequently, at airports). The con man shrewdly assesses the crowd, and when he spots a Bite Egg he falls into conversation with him, usually establishing himself by explaining that the two are traveling on the same train. He represents himself as a solid citizen from, say, Saskatchewan.

"You know," says the con man, "I'm on my way to my niece's wedding and I've had a very difficult time regarding her gift. Now out home I knew what she wanted all right: it's a silverware set—a Rogers 1870 called Lilac Time."

("We always go into these details," a member of the fraternity told me, "because the reaction you get from a man helps you a lot. It gives you an idea of how you're going along with him and how he's taking hold. If he's interested, you know you've got him.")

"Well, to order the gift I had to go into Saskatoon from Pumphandle. I went to Birks Jewellers there. Now, of course, there are seventy-seven pieces and I wanted her initials on each piece. That's considerable engraving and they couldn't do it in time for me to pick it up and take it with me on the train. I was going to cancel but they suggested they notify their Toronto store and while I was traveling they could do the work in Toronto and I could pick it up on arrival. When I got off the train this morning I had some breakfast and then went into the store. Doggone it, it wasn't ready!

"You know I've been back four times and I was getting real discouraged. They took pity on me and told me just to come back here to the depot and relax and they'd bring it down when it was ready. It's supposed to be ready by eight o'clock."

The con man always sets the time a few minutes before the train is to leave. At this point he breaks off and looks at his watch.

"By George, it's three minutes to eight now and I have a bill to change. If he's not here now, he will be by the time I break it."

Now comes the key to the wicked little game called the Bite. The con man has a newspaper folded under his arm.

"Just hold this for me, will you please," he says, handing the paper to the Egg. "I always make a hobby whenever I go on a trip of saving a newspaper from each place I've ever visited."

This simple action is called "conditioning." It establishes a bond of trust between the con man and the Egg.

"I'll be right back," says the con man. "Be sure to look after that paper." In about one minute he is back again.

"Well," he says in slight exasperation, taking the folded newspaper back from the Egg. "This is a new experience for me. I never had this happen before. It certainly couldn't happen out West."

"What's wrong?" asks the Egg. "Did you get it?"

"No. The messenger was there all right, but he didn't have the change and do you know?—these people here at the CNR refund and all those wickets won't change it! They just wouldn't accommodate me."

At this point the Egg usually offers to change the bill. If he doesn't, the con man says: "This poor old messenger must be about eighty-four. He really looks beat. I feel bad holding him up—he's been working overtime and I hate to keep him waiting. By George! It never struck me before, Mr. Smith, but would you happen to have change for a hundred-dollar bill?"

The Egg has.

"I should have thought of this before," says the con man, much relieved.

The Egg is now busily counting out ten tens or five twenties. "This is very good of you," says the con man. And he takes all the money.

At this point—and this is the key moment in the game—*he hands the newspaper back to the Egg.*

The psychologists, no doubt, will know exactly what transpires in the Egg's subconscious. Confidence men have had no professional psychological training, but they are masters of the practice. They have learned that this transfer of a ten-cent newspaper somehow gives the Egg confidence that the stranger will return.

As the con man hands over the newspaper, he says: "This is very decent of you, Mr. Smith. The messenger has the bill and the poor fellow is trying to get the change. I'll just intercept him and be right back. You just wait here, the same as before."

The con man, of course, has not revealed to the Egg that he himself does not have the hundred-dollar bill until he gets the Egg's money in his hand. Then, instead of handing him the mythical hundred-dollar bill he hands him the newspaper, which becomes a sort of substitute.

One con man told me that some Eggs think they are getting the bill with the newspaper and he has to spell it out for them: "No! No! I told you the messenger has the bill. I'll get it from him and be right back. Just wait there."

It is difficult to believe that anybody would give an utter stranger one hundred dollars in return for a ten-cent newspaper, but it has happened in thousands of cases. Once a man is sized up as a Bite Egg, the con fraternity seldom has any trouble with him.

The Egg rarely calls the police since he has a train to catch. He waits patiently as long as he dares and then climbs on board wondering what happened. So skillful are some con men that there have been Eggs who never realized they were cheated. They have abided forever in the belief that the nice stranger was somehow lost or delayed and—were there only a little more time—would have returned with all that money to reclaim his valuable newspaper.

3

Except that the names and occasional small details have had to be changed, the following strange story happened exactly as I relate it, in the city of Toronto, about ten years ago. It began when one Julius Steirhouse, a retired Montreal furrier, paid his first visit to the Queen City to investigate some stocks in which he was planning to invest his savings of $35,000.

Steirhouse booked into the King Edward hotel and then walked west on King Street, looking for the financial district. At the corner of Yonge he paused to get his bearings; an amiable stranger strolled up, asked if he could help, and directed him toward Bay Street. By coincidence, the stranger was going in the same direction and so the two men walked along together chatting as they went, stopping occasionally at the stranger's suggestion to look into the store windows and talk.

The stranger, whose name was Reg Johnstone, was cheerfully talkative. He told Steirhouse that he had just come into a bit of money through the sale of the family business. By another coincidence he was interested in some of the same stocks that Steirhouse was looking at; indeed he showed considerable knowledge of the market.

Alone in a strange city, Steirhouse warmed to him. Mr. Johnstone told him small, intimate secrets of his life, and the furrier soon found himself exchanging confidences—including the intelligence that he had $35,000 in negotiable securities in a safety-deposit box in Montreal. He was not to have it long.

Steirhouse could not know that he was about to be set up for the most ingenious and complicated of all modern confidence games, the Payoff. In North America, millions of dollars have been mulcted from gullible people through this one game. Though con men have gone to jail for playing it, the swindle is so carefully planned and executed that in case after case the culprits have never been apprehended.

Honed to a fine edge by generations of con men, the Payoff is as carefully rehearsed as a stage play. Since the rules and *modus operandi* are always the same, a good Payoff man can work anywhere in the world; and Reg Johnstone was a good Payoff man: he had once taken $100,000 from a victim in less than a week.

There is a saying in the half-world of the con fraternity that if you do not find an Egg, the Egg will find you, and Johnstone had been idling at the corner of King and Yonge, certain that one would soon come along. It had been his observation that one third of humanity was composed of Eggs. Johnstone was looking for an elderly, affluent stranger, and his shrewd eye, trained from twenty-five years' experience, easily picked out Julius Steirhouse.

The two new-found friends visited the stock exchange together, dined together that evening, and took in a movie. The following day they went sightseeing around town, and during the next three days they became inseparable. Mr. Johnstone, who was also from Montreal, said he was staying at a small, private hotel—he didn't reveal the address—and said he would try to get his new friend settled there, too.

There is a bench on the pedestrian island on University Avenue at Dundas and, as the two crossed the street one noon hour, Johnstone suggested they sit down to rest and have a smoke.

"Excuse me," he said, after they were seated. "I stepped on your foot!"

"No, you didn't," replied Steirhouse.

"Well, I stepped on *something*," said Johnstone, reaching down below him. "Hullo! What's this?"

He picked up a large and very expensive wallet. The two men examined it curiously, opened it, and found $1,000 inside.

"Better see who it belongs to," said Johnstone, pulling out several credit cards, some betting slips, and a membership card to a club called the Turf Exchange on Bay Street. He delved further and produced a folded clipping from a Chicago newspaper with a three-column headline and a photograph of a man named Webster.

The two read the clipping together. N. R. Webster, it developed, was something of a mystery man—a big plunger and horse bettor believed to be a key man in a large New York gambling syndicate warring with certain bookmakers. Webster was suspected of the practice known as "past posting," i.e., betting on a horse race after it was won. He had left Chicago, the clipping said, and appeared to be in trouble with the syndicate.

Johnstone, dipping once again into the wallet, pulled out a letter, on expensive stationery, from a man in New York. It was addressed to N. R. Webster.

"If it were not for my close friendship with your late father," the letter read, "I should never have interceded for you at the top. But you must not put me on the spot again. I must warn you that this Toronto posting represents your final chance with us and that, should you ever again use confidential information for your own financial gain, that will be the end of it. Surely you ought to be satisfied with a salary and commission position that equals that of the U.S. President. . . ."

"My God!" said the awed Johnstone. "We're on to something big!"

He was; but not in the way that poor Julius Steirhouse understood him to mean.

The Payoff has its own vernacular. The letter the two men had just read is known as the "bawl-out" letter, and it, together with the phony newspaper clipping and the other paraphernalia, had been printed the previous day by a four-man confidence ring in Toronto. Johnstone was known as the Steerer and it was his job to steer the Egg—Steirhouse—into the arms of the Player, Webster.

Across the street was a third member of the ring known as the Tail man. For the past fifteen minutes he had been examining the Egg closely. From this moment on, the Tail man, in various disguises, would never be far from Julius Steirhouse's side; it was important that the Egg should not slip through the gang's fingers. A fourth man would enter the elaborate play later in the day. All four would eventually split Mr. Steirhouse's $35,000.

The last item that Johnstone pulled from the mysterious wallet was a business card bearing the name of N. R. Webster, Esq., and giving, as an address, a suite at the Royal York Hotel. Johnstone steered his quarry to a phone booth and put in a call to Webster, the mystery man. Webster, told that the wallet had been found, sounded grateful but also suspicious. They weren't newspapermen, were they? Thank God! The press had almost ruined him in Chicago. Well, then, they must take a taxi to the hotel at once. But remember—no publicity! They must not even discuss the matter in front of the taxi driver!

In his Royal York suite, N. R. Webster, dripping affluence, was beside himself with gratitude.

"You'll have to forgive us for reading your personal papers," said Johnstone, repeating a phrase that he had used in dozens of previous Payoff games, "but we had to do it in order to identify you."

"That's perfectly all right, boys," Webster replied. "But for God's sake now, give me your promise you'll never mention any of this to a living soul. Now here—I want you to take $1,000 for your trouble."

"No! No!" cried Johnstone. "Honesty is a way of life with me. I don't do these things for reward. I wouldn't dream of taking your money, and I'm sure Mr. Steirhouse wouldn't either."

Steirhouse, flattered, nodded agreement. A good-humored argument followed.

"Well, look," said Johnstone finally, laughing. "If you really insist on doing something—put some money for us on the next horse you bet."

"I'll be happy to!" boomed Webster. "Mind you, I've never involved anyone else in this business before. I'm taking a big enough chance when I do it for my own benefit."

He paused and looked about, then dropped his voice: "You know, we're betting these horses after they win. We have a situation here where we can get a delay in the wired results to the bookies of five or ten minutes, depending on how much we want to pay. It costs us $1,000 a day for each minute of delay. Of course, the money comes from big Wall Street bankers. It's the principle of the thing they're interested in, not profits. They want to break the hold of these bookmakers who are bleeding the working man white—put them right out of business. But I don't mind telling you I've made a good thing out of this personally."

As he was speaking, Webster opened the window as if to get air. This was a signal for the Tail man to phone the room.

"Now I can't tell when there'll be another big one," Webster was saying as he raised the window. "But when it comes up, you can bet I'll let you boys in on it." The phone rang and he made a signal of dismissal as he moved to answer it. The Steer man began to edge the Egg from the room.

"Bye now!" waved Webster, picking up the phone. "I'll be in touch."

"Don't worry," whispered the Steer man as the two reached the door. "He's obviously a man of his word."

"Hold on a minute," Webster called as they were about to close the door. "We're in luck. A good one's just come up. Here, Johnstone: I want you to take this $1,000 and these credit slips and get right over to the Turf Exchange."

He pulled three small cards from his wallet. "I'm placing $1,000 for each of you to win on the next race and a couple of thousand for myself," Webster said. "I'll just get your names down here. Let me have your initials, will you, Johnstone: R.G.? Right. And yours, Steirhouse? J.S.? Fine."

But on the credit slip Webster reversed Steirhouse's initials to S. J. It is the kind of simple slip that many people make, but in the Payoff it is no mistake; it is in the script and it is the key to a colossal swindle.

"This admission card will get you into the Exchange," Webster said. "I'll call my chauffeur in the lobby and he'll take you over in the Cadillac. He'll be the man at the side door with the black uniform."

And so, after some further play-acting, the Steer man left the suite, to return presently, his eyes shining.

"You ought to see that place," he told the wide-eyed Steirhouse, referring to the fictional Turf Exchange. "It's absolutely fabulous. Why, they're betting hundreds of thousands. . . ."

The phone rang to inform Webster that his horse had won.

"Look, boys," Webster said. "There's another good one coming up. What do you say we bet our winnings?"

The three men bet twice more, and won each time. Finally Webster called a halt.

"That's all today, gentlemen. Not bad; we've won $140,000 between us. That's $70,000 for me and $35,000 apiece for you two. I'll have them deliver the cash right away."

He picked up the phone: "Hello, this is Webster. Yes, that's right. Will you bring it over, please? You know my suite. How long? Yes, I know it takes time, but no more than forty minutes, now. I have an engagement for the evening."

Half an hour later there was a rap on the door and the fourth member of the confidence ring, in the role of the bookmaker's messenger, arrived with a satchel that appeared to be loaded with money.

"Let's count it out," Webster was saying when the phone rang again: "Yes—he's just arrived. I'll let you speak to him" —and he turned the phone over to the messenger, who spoke briefly and hung up.

"I'm sorry, gentlemen," the fake messenger said, closing the satchel. "That was the manager of the Exchange. He's just learned that the major portion of this was a credit bet, and he's instructed me not to issue the money until you can show evidence that you were financially able to pay in case of a loss."

"What do we have to do?" Webster asked.

"You'll have to show that you could have paid $140,000 in order to win that much. It's a strict rule at the Exchange."

"How long have we got?"

The messenger made another call: "Forty-eight hours—no more," he said.

Then he left.

"Oh, well," said Webster, with relief. "That's no trouble really. I haven't got that much cash here, but I certainly can get $70,000 within a day. I have to be very careful, you know, not to excite suspicion, but I'll have my brother wire it to my bank here. He's in Mexico."

He turned to Johnstone: "What's the most you can raise

without discussing it with anybody?—and I mean *anybody:* not even your wife!"

"Well, I've got $35,000 in cash in a safety-deposit box in Montreal," the Steer man replied.

"Let's see: that gives us $105,000. We're still short. Well, it's no use. I just can't lay my hands on any more without causing suspicion. I guess we'll have to forget it."

"Wait!" said Steirhouse, coming in on cue. "I could get the rest, I think."

"That's right," said Johnstone. "Mr. Steirhouse is no bum, you know, Mr. Webster. He's a man of substantial means."

"How can you get it?" Webster wanted to know, suspicion in his voice. "You can't go to anybody you know."

"I can cash my securities in Montreal and transfer the funds to the bank here," Steirhouse told him eagerly.

"Well, all we've got to do is show that the money's on account here in town and we'll be paid," said Webster. "It's just a formality with the Exchange. They'll be quite happy to pay if we can each show substantial accounts."

It is important to note here that Steirhouse had no reason to believe his money was in jeopardy since he would not be required to draw it from the bank but only to show a slip confirming that it was on deposit. It is also significant that, with a fortune apparently in his grasp, he did not question the arithmetic or the logic of this preposterous proposition. He was, in short, acting like all Eggs at this stage of the Payoff game. (The writer has been assured by con artists that, by the time this act in the play is reached, no Egg ever backs down, questions the set-up, or calls his new-found friends liars, swindlers, or cheats. He has put his confidence in the Steer man, and he acts like a lover who believes his beloved is ever true. He is, in short, mesmerized.)

Off went Julius Steirhouse to Montreal with the ever-present Johnstone, who also was supposed to be raising $35,-

ooo but whose real purpose was to keep the Egg warmed up and in a relaxed frame of mind.

Two days later, the charade was resumed in Webster's Royal York suite. Back came the messenger with his satchel full of bills. But now a second hitch developed. Steirhouse's credit slip, it turned out, bore the wrong name.

"I'm sorry," said the messenger. "My instructions are to pay S. J. Steirhouse. The name on the bank slip is J. S. Steirhouse. I just can't pay you."

"Well, there's only one thing to do, then," said Webster briskly, standing up. "We've only a very short time left and we're going to have to move quickly. We'll have to draw our cash from the bank and bring it back here to show our good faith." With that, he hustled the other two from the room before the Egg had time to think.

And that is how Julius Steirhouse came to draw $35,000 in cash from the bank in Montreal and take it in a neat bundle to the Royal York—with a Tail man walking carefully in his wake every step of the way.

Back in the suite the two con men also produced neat packages of what appeared to be money. Each placed his money in a brief case and then Webster, always in complete charge, gave Johnstone orders to go to the mythical Turf Exchange for the cash.

"They'll have no out this time," he said. Then, as an afterthought: "Oh, Johnstone—just before you go. Here's a betting slip for my share. Place my money here, will you?"—and he indicated the betting slip.

Reg Johnstone, Steer man extraordinary, was a consummate actor, as all good con men must be. When he returned, forty minutes later, he gave one of his finest performances, using only two props—the betting slip and the brief case, now empty of cash.

He entered the room, almost in tears, and Webster in dismay asked what was wrong.

"Oh, my God, I could kill myself!" Johnstone cried. "I don't know what happened. I was only trying to do the best for everybody. You told me we were betting on sure winners. I can't understand what went wrong."

"What are you talking about?" cried Webster, seizing him by the lapels. "What have you done?"

"Well, I put your share on this horse, like you told me, and then . . . I put ours on, too, thinking the horse had won. Why didn't it win?"

"You idiot!" cried Webster, seizing the betting slip. "I told you to *place* that bet! Here it is, plain as day. Don't you know what place means? There's a win, a place, and a show —first, second, and third. Of course we can't keep betting on winners; the Exchange wouldn't accept it. We have to take the occasional place and show horse. I thought you had normal intelligence, but you turn out to be an utter idiot. By God, Johnstone, I could kill you. Here—Steirhouse—open that window—"

"Please! Please!" cried Steirhouse, fearing trouble. Webster pretended to calm down.

"Now, look, Steirhouse—none of this is your fault and as far as I'm concerned you haven't lost a thing. We'll fix that up. But this man has got to go. I suppose he made an honest mistake, but I won't suffer fools around me. I only wish I'd sent you over, Steirhouse, and not this idiot. Johnstone: I want you to get out before I get really angry. Don't ever bother me again. And if I ever hear that you've breathed a word of this I'll see you're taken care of—and I don't mean the police; I have other connections."

Johnstone by this time was crying real tears. (It wasn't difficult. He had put in a tense five days to get that $35,000 and the excitement of the game had kept his emotions on edge.) Steirhouse felt so badly for his friend that he actually put his arms around him and promised that he'd split anything he made with him.

"Don't worry—I know you meant the best for us," Steirhouse said as Johnstone left, and Johnstone, hearing this, realized that this Egg would not be difficult to cool out.

The most important part of the Payoff game now followed: the process of cooling Steirhouse out so that he would not suspect anything crooked and go to the police.

"Don't worry," said Webster, after Johnstone left. "I'm going to look after you. In fact, you may be very useful to me as a front man. Here's the name of a hotel in Boston. Go there immediately and check in under the name of Monroe. I'll be in touch with you there."

Steirhouse, trailed to the train by the Tail man, did exactly what he was told. After a day in the Boston hotel, he received a long-distance call from Webster telling him to go to New York to another hotel and register under another name. In New York, Steirhouse was sent to Chicago. From Chicago he was sent to Minneapolis. The purpose of this was twofold: first, to tire Steirhouse out; second, to make any story to the police sound highly suspicious.

By the time he reached Minneapolis, the weary Steirhouse was pleading to be allowed to go home. When the gang decided he was sufficiently cool, Webster phoned him again. "The heat's on me," he said. "The syndicate has caught on to what I've been doing, and I'm in trouble. We'll have to wait until this thing blows over; but don't worry—I'll be in touch with you. You'd better go back to Montreal. I should be able to get things going again in ninety days."

And so Julius Steirhouse, $35,000 poorer, returned to Montreal, and never again heard from Mr. Webster or Mr. Johnstone. For the rest of his life he believed all the hokum he had been told. He died a short time ago without ever suspecting that he had been the victim of one of the cleverest swindles in the world.

3

Millie and the Song Sharks

Mrs. Millie Pilipovic is a pretty and petite young housewife whose husband is a steelworker in the big industrial town of Hamilton, Ontario. Like so many other women who read the fan magazines and listen to the top fifty tunes on the radio, she had for years dreamed of writing a hit song herself. It did not seem too difficult, considering some of the trash the disc jockeys were playing; and the ads for songwriters were always saying how badly new songs were needed. Mrs. Pilipovic decided to give it a try and all her friends encouraged her.

In December 1958 Mrs. Pilipovic's dreams seemed to be fulfilled when the Toronto *Daily Star* carried her picture and a four-column headline reading HAMILTON MOTHER ON

HIT PARADE. The feature story beneath it appeared to tell the tale.

SPECIAL TO THE STAR

Hamilton, Dec. 8—Turned down by Canadian recording companies, two tunes written and composed by a young Hamilton housewife have been released in the U.S. and are on the Hit Parade in several states.

"Dreamy Melody," and "I'm Sad and Blue," words and music by Millie Pilipovic, 24, of Gertrude St., are being released in Canada today. They have been selling by the thousands in the U.S.

And it only took Millie eight minutes to write the words and compose the music for both tunes, one a Western ballad, the other a waltz.

The brunette mother of a six-year-old son, who plays no instrument and never had a music lesson, said she literally dreamed her first tune.

"I dreamed of the melody and words of my first recording all one night," she said. "When I awoke in the morning they were still fresh in my mind.

"I got a pencil and paper and had the words and music down within five minutes."

Mrs. Pilipovic told of sending her tunes to song publishers and recording companies all over Canada. "They were all turned down flat," she said.

"That's why I sent them to a Hollywood recording company. I got a reply a week after I sent them. I could have wept for joy, both tunes had been accepted."

"Dreamy Melody" was recorded by the "Madhatters," and "I'm Sad and Blue," by cowboy balladeer Slim Dallas, and they're now being distributed all over North America.

"I'm sorry that it was not a Canadian company that released my tunes," the housewife-songwriter sighed, "but it wasn't for the lack of trying."

She said the biggest obstacle she met here in Hamilton and Toronto was getting radio disc jockeys to listen to her tunes.

"They just weren't interested," she said, "so I sent them to the U.S. company. They liked them and that was it."

About the future, Millie Pilipovic is confident.

"I have a few tunes lilting around in my head I think are

much better than 'Dreamy Melody,' and I'll be settling down to write them shortly."

"My ambition is to compose a top tune that will sell over 1,000,000 records," Millie said, "that's what I aim to do."

The story was planted (as we shall learn later); but Mrs. Pilipovic's friends, who rushed to congratulate her, could not know that. Letters and phone calls poured in. Several other would-be songwriters wrote to send along their lyrics and to ask her advice. Mrs. Pilipovic replied cheerfully to them all, explaining that they would need a Hollywood agent and a publisher and giving them the names of the ones she had used.

"I have two royalty contracts, but if you have songs, don't send them to the publishing firms," she wrote one inquirer. "Have an agent do that for you, as they only accept professional work. . . . I wouldn't have got this far if it hadn't been for people helping me from the States. . . . As for success, I'd say I had it as far as I could go it alone. My co-writer, Yodelling Slim Dallas, had to wait four years, and he plays instruments, etc., before he could get a start, and look where he is today. . . ."

How could this optimistic and long-struggling housewife know that very little in that news story was true? that no radio station in her neighborhood or anywhere else was featuring her records? that the Madhatters and Slim Dallas were virtual unknowns, without stature in the industry? that her songs were not selling at all? that none had made the Hit Parade and that none had any chance of making the Hit Parade?

What the news story did not say was that Mrs. Pilipovic had paid to have her songs published. Perhaps it was worth the money. She reveled in her small hour of glory. Disillusionment was still several months away.

2

When I read the story about Millie Pilipovic, I filed it for future reference, for I was, at that moment, conducting a small experiment of my own.

I have always been attracted by the advertisements in the back pages of the fan magazines; it seems to me that they tell a great deal about the secret yearnings of a good chunk of North American womanhood. There are ads telling women how to enlarge their busts and ads for perfumes that are supposed to drive young men insensate and ads for falsies to wear on the buttocks. But the ads that interested me most were these:

SONGS
INTO DOLLARS!
NEW songwriters, poets share $33 million
yearly.   Songs composed.   PUBLISHED
Promoted.   Appraisal, infor.   FREE from
Nordyke Music Publishers
6000 Sunset
Hollywood 2813
Calif.

I decided one day to write a poem under my nine-year-old daughter's name—as sloppy and as mediocre a poem as I had the wit to compose—and send it in to all three addresses for the free appraisal. With it I enclosed a covering letter.

DEAR SIRS:

I saw your ad in this month's "Screen Stars" mag.

I write love poems as a hobby and some of my girl friends say I should get them published.

Please let me know if there is any use me trying this. I hear there is money in it but that publishers steal songs.

But is my song GOOD enough?

I enclose a sample.

Yours sincerely,
Penny Berton

Here was the sample:

IN THE DARK
By Penny Berton
In the dark, when you're near
I'm loving you dear
And though no one can hear
Us, I fear
You don't love me.

Is this because
There's been a pause
In our friendship?
Could it be
You don't love me
    And this is the end-ship?

CHORUS: Say it's not true
For I love you
Honest, I do!
You know I do!

It is fairly easy to write a mediocre song-poem, but it is not so easy to write a really terrible one. I felt, however, that the cunning rhyming of "friendship" with "end-ship" would serve to disqualify this one. I was wrong.

Every author, amateur or professional, gets a small tingle in his spine when something he has created is accepted with enthusiasm. And enthusiasm is the only word to use for the ecstatic letter I quickly received from Mr. John White of the Nordyke Music Publishing Co. Mr. White is one of those people who cannot contain himself when he is really excited. Like Queen Victoria, he underlines words for emphasis. When that isn't enough, he moves into upper case, and when *that* isn't enough, he underlines the upper case. He is the only publisher I have ever dealt with who does this.

Here is Mr. White's letter:

DEAR MISS BERTON:

Thank you for submitting your lyric for Free appraisal. Our Professional Staff unanimously agrees your song material indicates a NEW, GENUINE and ORIGINAL TALENT worthy of OUR IMMEDIATE PUBLICATION.

NORDYKE Music Publishing Co. is the world's largest Music Publisher specializing in the DISCOVERY & PROMOTION of the creative works of ALL amateur and unknown Song-writers & Songpoets. We have started to fame and wealth many hundreds of people like *YOU* who have PUBLISHED with us.

NORDYKE Music Publishing Co. will PUBLISH for YOU your excellent work for which will be created at NO extra charge by a famous, successful Composer, a BEAUTIFUL MELODY and PIANO ARRANGEMENT. When payment is completed of $110.00 for each song, that song will be quickly PUBLISHED and widely PROMOTED. Enclosed SONG PUBLISHING & ROYALTY PAYMENT CONTRACTS plus other important forms to be completed and promptly returned.

Thank you for the privilege of allowing NORDYKE Music Publishing Co. to help YOU to your well-deserved FAME, SUCCESS and WEALTH. Please submit for FREE appraisal more of your best Songs and Songpoems.

YOUR PUBLISHER,
NORDYKE Music Publishing Co.
John White

IMPORTANT: Our MONTHLY QUOTA is rapidly nearing capacity of NEW songs for RECORDS, TELEVISION, RADIO, MOTION PICTURES, SHOWS, ENTERTAINERS, etc. *YOUR* song will be included in this PUBLICATION group if you *promptly* accept our wonderful offer. YOU will forever be happy you PUBLISHED your song.

That same week I received equally encouraging letters from the other two publishers:

Larry Allen, president of Crown Music, wrote me a personally mimeographed letter. He and his staff had carefully examined my lyrics and wanted to start me at once on the road to FAME and FORTUNE. The price for collaborating with me was only $39, and Mr. Allen later wrote me reducing that price to $34 if I ACTED PROMPTLY.

Mr. Allen's qualifications were impressive. He had a degree in music "from one of the largest Universities in the Country," which he modestly did not name. He had been a member of the staff of the music department "of a large Eastern college," which he modestly did not name. He had composed the score for "a very successful musical comedy show," which he modestly did not name. Mr. Allen's modesty was exceeded only by his great talent.

I wrote Mr. Allen a second letter asking him if he really thought my song was good enough to publish. His answer was slightly guarded. "We accept only poems that we feel are good material for songs," he said. "Your poem contains good ideas and we can make a very nice song out of it."

J. Chas. McNeil, Master of Music, wrote that my poem "should make an excellent song," and, as he says he always gives "a frank and candid opinion," this was exciting news. Mr. McNeil's price was $45, but his qualifications were superb —even better than Mr. Allen's. He had actually won Awards. He had actually written Famous Songs such as *I Salute You, Darling.*

All three companies sent me standard contracts. All I had to do was sign my name and launch myself on a new career. I resisted the urge and, instead, published the song and all the correspondence in my newspaper column. I did so with very little comment, since it seemed to me the facts spoke for themselves.

I was horrified, the following day, to get a series of phone calls and letters from various people, mainly housewives, asking for the addresses of these three music companies. "My song's every bit as good as the one you sent in," one woman told me on the phone. "In fact, I think it's a lot better. If they were willing to publish yours, I think there's got to be a chance for mine."

After that, I began to wonder about the song I had written. Perhaps it really *was* publishable. I decided to try to write a worse song, which I submitted to a fourth Hollywood company, Five-Star Music Makers. This purported to come from my seven-year-old daughter.

WANTCHA
By Pamela Berton
Wantcha, wantcha, wantcha, wantcha, wantcha,
wantcha, wantcha, wantcha, wantcha, wantcha,
wantcha, wantcha
    all the time.
Needta, needta, needta, needta, needta,
needta, needta, needta, needta, needta,
needta, needta
    make you mine.

This song, too, was accepted almost instantaneously for publication. I was told that all I had to do was sign a contract and send money. At this point I thought it pertinent to get in touch with Millie Pilipovic, whose success story had appeared in my own newspaper. That story sounded suspiciously like the reprints from home-town newspapers sent out with the enthusiastic acceptance letter by the Nordyke Music Publishing Company to show how widely its writers' songs were promoted.

3

Several months had elapsed since the newspaper publicity had appeared when I visited Mrs. Pilipovic in her upstairs flat in Hamilton. She is a cheerful, warm-hearted woman, who obviously believes the best of everybody. Although no royalties had yet arrived from the music publishers who had accepted her songs, only the mildest of suspicions had crossed her mind.

But after hearing her story and reading the thick sheaf of correspondence, I had to tell her that she had very little chance of receiving a nickel. She had spent $82.50 getting one song published and $199 on another—a great deal of money to her. All she had to show for this investment was a couple of records, some badly printed sheets of music, and a songbook, produced by the offset process, containing one of her compositions.

Her songs had not sold in the thousands or even the hundreds; they had not sold at all. No hit parade had played her music, although one song, *I'm Sad and Blue*, had been played on a Mexican station at midnight by Yodelling Slim Dallas, so he could tell Mrs. Pilipovic the song had been played. Mrs. Pilipovic was a little bewildered by it all.

Mrs. Pilipovic's song-publishing career began in 1957 when she answered a magazine ad by Music Makers, in Hollywood, and submitted to them the lyrics for *Dreamy Melody:*

> *We were waltzing together*
> *To a dreamy melody*
> *As you whispered your sweet love to me*
> *Somehow I knew that our love could never be.*
> *We were waltzing together*
> *To our dreamy melody*
> *When she came and stole my love from me.*
> *And as both of you waltzed away*
> *Then I knew that I could never never stay*
> *As you waltzed together*
> *To our dreamy melody.*

On April 6, Mrs. Pilipovic received this mimeographed *Report on Song Material* from Music Makers.

We have examined the song material mentioned below and wish to advise you that it meets with our requirements. We recommend it for immediate production as we feel these lyrics can be developed in an appealing manner. We wish to assure you of our sincere efforts on this material, if you place it with us, and feel that it is worthy of your efforts as well as ours.

Music Makers agreed to supply music for the song, to have it recorded "using professional Hollywood talent," and to supply ten "manuscript lead sheet copies," all for $28. It seemed like a bargain to Mrs. Pilipovic, who signed the contract and paid the money. In return, she was sent ten photostatic reproductions of her song, printed by hand, suitable for playing on the piano with one finger. She received, in addition, a record containing several songs, one of which was hers, sung by a single male vocalist with piano accompaniment. The vocalist, according to the letter from Sydney Freed, managing director of Music Makers, was somebody named Gil Dagenais: "He is quite well known around here, as he has sung in such famous places as the Macomba, Ciro's, and the Beverly Hills Hotel Crystal Room."

Mrs. Pilipovic got something else for her $28. She got on the Hollywood sucker list. All that year she received come-on letters from various people and institutions whose business it is to make a profit from people who daydream about writing hit songs.

The most enticing piece of mail arrived on July 15, 1957. The letterhead was impressive, since it suggested an enormous production enterprise with studios scattered all over Hollywood:

RALPH E. HASTINGS
Producers Motion Picture Studios
Studio Three
5634 Santa Monica Blvd.
Hollywood 38, Calif.

The letter was a personal one and, as with all of Mr. Hastings's future correspondence, it had a crisp, authentic ring to it. There were no words capitalized or underlined. There were no exclamation points. The letter had the air of one professional talking to another on equal terms. It is worth reproducing in full.

Dear Mrs. Pilipovic:

The Madhatters have informed me that they are willing to record your song with orchestra at a session now being scheduled and have requested that I contact you for the necessary permission. I am the Madhatters' personal manager.

As I understand, the song which the Madhatters refer to is one of your compositions they learned of from a publisher's agent who is either handling your song or has handled it in the past. The title of the composition is "DREAMY MELODY."

The master audition recording will be retained here at the Producers Motion Picture Studios, Studio Three, but we will, of course, for your files forward a copy of the recording to you. The Madhatters will sing the vocal and be accompanied by the Studio Three orchestra. In the event I negotiate for motion picture use, you will be required to pay me ten percent of any monies received for allowing the song to be used in a motion picture.

Representing the Madhatters, I am, of course, equally interested in the development of the music they use that is recorded through Studio Three.

Mrs. Pilipovic, I am sure you will grant your permission allowing the Madhatters to record the song, when I say that in my opinion they are the finest group of recording artists I have handled in many years. Some of the top stars of motion pictures applauded them over and over and call them "terrific" and "definitely one of the finest."

For the recording session we will need two more copies of the song, an orchestra arrangement and a vocal arrangement for the Madhatters. I am enclosing recording and agent agreements which must be signed before we can proceed. Upon your agreement of percentages under the terms of the enclosed contracts, we will notify you as to the style of orchestration you are to forward, outlining the different instruments in the orchestra and the style of vocal arrangement best suited to the style of the Madhatters.

If you do not have an orchestration and vocal arrangement of the song, or if you find any difficulty in obtaining them, advise me by airmail and I will attempt to make the arrangements here. However, it will be absolutely necessary that you forward me one or two copies of the song.

Millie Pilipovic was flattered by this attention. Of course, she did not have the orchestra or vocal arrangements; she had not written a note of music in her life. Mr. Hastings had said he would "attempt" to make the arrangements in Hollywood. Since the Madhatters seemed so desperate for her song, Mrs. Pilipovic wrote an airmail letter asking him to make the attempt.

The attempt was successful. Mr. Hastings replied that "the Director of Recording has been informed of your advice that no orchestration or vocal arrangement is available. He advised that he can have the necessary arrangements prepared for both the Studio orchestra and the Madhatters. The Studio Three scale rate for both the orchestration and the vocal arrangement will be $77.50. This includes any special melody and harmony instrument features and the Madhatter solos if written in feature." Mr. Hastings further asked that Mrs. Pilipovic send in, with her check or money order, a note explaining what it was for: "This in the event I am not at the studio at the time of arrival, and will enable one of my assistants to proceed with the session schedule without further delay."

The thing that impressed Mrs. Pilipovic, apart from all the trade jargon about "session schedule" and "harmony instrument features," was how inexpensive it all was. She could not raise all the money right away but was able to send it in two installments over the next two months. In September she received, for her $77.50, a small 45-rpm disc containing her song and three others, all by unknowns. She played it for me, and there is only one word to describe the performance given by the famous Studio Three orchestra and that fine group of recording artists, the Madhatters: dismal.

On October 24, the helpful Mr. Hastings wrote another of his soft-sell letters.

Dear Mrs. Pilipovic:

As we both understand, you are not required or obligated to expend any further monies for the development specified in the agreement which covers the recording by the Madhatters, and the availability of that recording to motion pictures, television, and radio.

The song has been recorded by the Madhatters and is in our opinion a very fine recording. If successfully placed in a picture, the Madhatters recording could assist the song on the road toward success.

This letter is for the purpose of advising you that if you desire to have the recording pressed on commercial records, and distributed to certain key disc jockeys, and at the same time advertised to record stores, we can make the necessary contacts to have this done. . . .

I have been asked by several writers, who have a Madhatter recording of their song, to check on costs of manufacturing commercial records, which I have done, and for the purpose of information, I am conveying this to you in the event you desire that commercial records be prepared for "DREAMY MELODY."

To put out the popular 45-rpm speed, using two songs on each side of the record (which is popular in view of the 45-rpm speed), we can have the masters, stampers and pressings completed, pressing an original 100 records, at a cost to you of $94.00.

After the original 100 records are pressed, we plan to contact disc jockeys and record stores. We will then send the selected disc jockeys a recording and the music stores a notice that commercial records of the song are ready and available to be put on sale. The record manufacturer is then in a position to fill orders at the standard wholesale rate.

In reference to royalties, you are to be entitled to 90% and we to 10% of any royalty money paid by the record company in the event of paid-for sales.

If you desire that this be done, kindly advise.

Mrs. Pilipovic did not have the $94 and so had to let the opportunity pass. But Mr. Hastings didn't give up. On December 11, he tried another tack.

Dear Mrs. Pilipovic:
Studio Three is preparing the yearly holiday salutation greetings that we send to major recording companies, selected big-name recording artists, and important music publishers. I have an idea to further the presentation of the fine Madhatter recording of "DREAMY MELODY."

I would like to have this song printed on a full-size, well-designed Christmas and New Year greeting and included in the Christmas mailing from Studio Three to the above-mentioned important recorders and publishers.

I have checked costs with the artist who designs the Christmas cards and also with the printer. I would want to have no less than 250 prepared.

Inasmuch as the mailing can go with the regular Studio Three holiday greeting mailing, the cost to you, to include the song, would run $32.00.

In view of the time element, it will be necessary that you reply within the next week. My plan is that the song be printed in full on one side of the greeting and bear the notice that the Madhatters have recorded this number.

Please reply in the enclosed airmail envelope as time is of the essence.

Again, Mrs. Pilipovic had to refuse. She did not have the money. But on February 11, 1958, Mr. Hastings wrote her another of his crisply professional-sounding letters, and this one excited her interest. It came on a new and jazzier letterhead, and from a new address. It did not mention a motion-picture studio; it was "Ralph E. Hastings, Recording Management" this time, "currently featuring the Madhatters, Ken Starr, the Vincent Poli Orchestra."

Dear Mrs. Pilipovic:

It is my desire to handle hits. My opinion is that songs recorded by as fine a group as are the Madhatters deserve public attention. Many producers of motion picture musicals and leading recording companies prefer to consider published music. In spite of the fact that my contract with you is specifically representation of the record, I believe an attempt should be made to try to obtain a publishing contract.

With this in mind and with your permission, I plan to enter into conversations with publishers.

Many of the top recording artists and important recording companies prefer that a song be published before they negotiate a royalty contract.

In the event any discussions I may have with publishers develop an interest on their part, I will advise you. I feel that the fact that we have a Madhatter recording should develop interest on the part of publishers.

I plan to negotiate with active, responsible publishing companies, on a basis where they, the publishers, pay all costs of publishing under a standard royalty contract.

I will make no commitment until I advise you of any offers that might develop and secure your approval.

Two weeks after she received this letter, Mrs. Pilipovic received from Mr. Hastings, in Beverly Hills, a wire which left her breathless.

DREAMY MELODY ACCEPTED BY PUBLISHING FIRM ON STAND-ARD ROYALTY CONTRACT. WE MUST MANUFACTURE COMMER-CIAL TYPE RECORDS TO COVER PUBLISHER'S DISC JOCKEY CON-TRACTS. PUBLISHER WILL ISSUE ROYALTY PUBLICATION CON-TRACTS DIRECT TO YOU WHEN I GUARANTEE HIM RECORDS ARE BEING MANUFACTURED. RECORD MANUFACTURER ASSURES ME FAST SERVICE. PUBLISHER READY TO GO TO PRESS WHEN REC-ORDS SHIPPED TO DISC JOCKEYS. I CHECKED PUBLISHERS ROY-ALTY CONTRACT, CARRIES STANDARD TERMS, ALL PUBLICA-TION DISTRIBUTION EXPENSES NOW AND IN FUTURE PAID BY PUBLISHER. AS PREVIOUSLY ADVISED, THE COST TO YOU FOR THE RECORDS WILL RUN $94. IF NECESSARY, CAN START PRE-LIMINARY MANUFACTURING STEPS WITH $50. ADVISE ME BY AIRMAIL.

In Millie Pilipovic's mind this was too good an offer to turn down; she dispatched a check for $50 to Mr. Hastings by re-

turn mail. He replied that he was "ordering the preliminary
master to ultimately press 100 commercial type records" and
"notifying the publisher that the records are in process and
requesting that he prepare the royalty publication contracts."

"In my opinion," wrote Mr. Hastings, "we have the Madhatters to thank for the publisher's approval. He is very impressed with their abilities."

Late in March Mrs. Pilipovic raised the additional $44.
She received a standard royalty contract from Eagle Pass
Music Publications and a little later a mimeographed form
letter saying that it might be some months before her song
was published, asking her to be patient about that, and adding that she would receive a free complimentary copy in due
course. The letter went on:

> We are very busy here and do not have time to answer
> unnecessary correspondence. . . .
> If you do not receive a royalty check and statement . . .
> do not become alarmed. It simply means that NO royalties
> are due. We are doing our level best to sell copies of your
> published song. . . . The only possible way that we can
> recover our investment is IF the song is accepted by the
> public and SELLS. . . . Remember that we have your
> name and address on file. If anything develops on your
> song, you will hear from US. It is not necessary that you
> write us as you will receive your check and statement IF
> and WHEN any royalties are due you. . . . Do not flood
> our office with unnecessary correspondence. . . . Do not
> become alarmed. . . .

Eventually Mrs. Pilipovic received a cheaply produced
pamphlet, published by the offset process from typewritten
material, titled *Bud Moore's Hillbilly Jamboree Songs*. It
contained the words of thirty-two songs, all by amateurs,

including *Dreamy Melody*, with enough music to allow anybody to play it on the piano with one finger. This pamphlet,
published by Eagle Pass, had the price $1.25 stamped in
large letters on the cover. Bud Moore, whose picture appeared within, was listed as "The King of Country Comedy,"
broadcasting on a radio station out of Clearfield, Pennsyl-
vania.

Shortly after that, Mrs. Pilipovic got another mimeographed letter from Eagle Pass urging her to buy, at a reduced rate of twenty-five cents a copy, one hundred books
containing her song. The suggestion was that she could make
big money peddling them to her friends, but Mrs. Pilipovic
resisted the offer, and that was the last she heard from Eagle
Pass.

And that is all Mrs. Pilipovic got for her total expenditure
of $199: two bad records, ten useless pieces of sheet music,
and one booklet. Mr. Hastings was shortly to bow out of the
picture, too, but before he did he tried one more letter.

Dear Mrs. Pilipovic:
You are familiar with the quality of Madhatter recordings. You are further familiar with the fact that as a result
of the Madhatter recordings, I was able to interest a publisher and obtain a standard royalty contract.

There is a possibility that other commitments might
keep the Madhatters from being available to me for recording sessions in the near future. There has been some
talk that the group may go on tour. In the event that you
have other songs that might fit the style of the Madhatters
and you desire the opportunity offered by the Madhatters
for such other compositions, we suggest you send them to
us at your earliest convenience.

But Mrs. Pilipovic, who by then was paying out money to
Yodelling Slim Dallas, didn't take advantage of the offer. The

following February she received the following kiss-off from Mr. Hastings, whose letterhead showed that he had changed his address for the third time in less than two years.

> Inasmuch as your song, recorded by the Hastings Company, has been placed under publication contract in which you have transferred certain rights to the publisher, the six-months percentage recording contract executed by you and R. E. Hastings is automatically terminated.
>
> With our understanding and agreement, you were allowed to enter into a publishing contract with the publisher in spite of our 10% recording right. We no longer are entitled to the 10% and hereby relinquish same.
>
> In view of the fact that the song is now under publication contract, all further negotiations and correspondence should be handled directly between you and your publisher.

In short, Mrs. Pilipovic had nowhere to address any complaints since Mr. Hastings was no longer associated with her, and Eagle Pass, having fulfilled its agreement, was not answering any mail.

Yet Mr. Hastings had done exactly what he promised to do—no more and no less. It was just that he didn't really promise very much.

4

The story of Mrs. Pilipovic's dealings with Yodelling Slim Dallas differs only in degree. Yodelling Slim's full name is Dallas E. Turner, and he was listed as president of Eagle Pass Music Publications on the booklet that Mrs. Pilipovic received. However, in all her long correspondence with Yodelling Slim no mention of Eagle Pass was ever made.

The thing that impressed Millie Pilipovic about Yodelling Slim was that he pointedly refrained from asking for money when he offered to collaborate with her on a song. The letter, which addressed her as "Dear Millie," was written chattily, and she probably was unaware that it was mimeographed.

> You most likely have been paying to have your poems set to music. So many non-professional writers do this. Being a recognized writer and successful composer, the poems I select are set to music on standard terms. If I work with you the melody will be composed for 50% of any royalties that might develop under the terms of the standard royalty publishing contract.
>
> Consider this letter an invitation. You may airmail me several of your poems. . . . I'll look them over and give you an opinion. Quite a few professional writers are teaming up with new writers. Some of the biggest money earning songs have been developed from the ideas, poems and music of writers who never before had a hit.
>
> My publishers have asked me to submit new songs of various types such as popular, novelty, patriotic, western and also sacred. . . . If I place your song with a publisher, it will be with a publisher who does NOT charge for publication. . . . A publisher who meets the terms of a standard royalty publishing contract. . . .

This was more like it. Mrs. Pilipovic sent a copy of another song she'd written, called *I'm Sad and Blue,* and later heard that Yodelling Slim had accepted it. It was not until December 8, 1958, that he wrote to ask for money. Of all the letters Mrs. Pilipovic received from "your cowboy buddy," as he called himself, this was the only one that was not mimeographed.

Dear Millie:

I'm flying to Fort Worth, Wednesday the 10th. I'll be at the Hilton Hotel. My plane arrives at 8:37 Central Standard Time. The publisher who met my terms for the publication of our song is flying in to meet me. He is a member of B.M.I. and heads three publishing firms. I am placing certain of my songs with him and our song was among those he is willing to sign up. He has agreed to all royalty terms, and I've written into the contracts, "publication within 60 days." He has agreed.

The reason for the Fort Worth meeting is to make arrangements for a Radio broadcast of our song over Radio XEG, the powerful 100,000-watt clear-channel station known as the "Voice of North America." The publisher insists on radio introduction of our song and is adding that stipulation to our Standard Royalty Contract. If we introduce the song over XEG Radio, he will sign the contracts and commence publication and distribution.

I'll have to arrange to re-record the song for Radio. The publisher wants it announced on the Radio when the song is introduced—that it is recorded and that publication is underway. That both records and published copies will be available for requests by disc jockeys and entertainers within 30 to 60 days.

Millie, I have been a member of the A.F.M. (Musicians' Union) for many years and the union has set the scale for an artist member to record. The scale for just one person to make a recording, not counting studio time, materials and recording fees, is $82.50. I have already held one recording session and at my expense. I composed the melody to make the song a complete words and music composition. I've secured a publication commitment by a publisher recognized by B.M.I. So far, I've handled all expense in an effort to get the song started in the right way. To give it the opportunity of going over and the chance of making us both some money. The re-recording for Radio talent expense you should handle. This is only fair. I may hire talent or do the job myself, but in either event, I will hold your expense to a maximum of the $82.50. This is the union scale for a member session. As for the Radio costs, that depends on the amount of time purchased and as I want the publisher to be a guest on the broadcast, it may run a little more than my expectations. Whatever it runs, I will pay it.

My expenses in flying in to meet and entertain the publisher I will pay. Millie, I do expect you to take care of the one item and that is the new Radio recording wanted by the publisher. He promises to "Carry the Ball" from there on and neither you nor I are required to spend another cent on the song once he takes over.

Here are my plans: I'll meet the publisher at the Hilton Hotel, Wednesday evening (I believe his plane gets in at 10:50). I'll assure him of the XEG broadcast and get his signature on our Royalty Contracts. I'll then go into conference and arrange all Radio broadcast details. I'll advise you by wire or letter from Fort Worth when all details are settled, and the date and time of our song's broadcast.

If we are to place the song with a publisher, I will expect your wire or airmail money order in the amount of $82.50 to reach me at the Hilton Hotel, Fort Worth, Texas, at once. I will be with the publisher two or three days at the most.

This letter, with its explicitness regarding plane schedules and its sincerity of phraseology, was impressive. Millie Pilipovic sent the $82.50 to Fort Worth. Some days later, a mimeographed letter informed her that her song would be played on the Mexican station across the border between midnight and one a.m., January 30, 1959. From this point on, she continued to receive mail from Yodelling Slim addressed to "my wonderful friend," all of it mimeographed and almost all of it full of schemes that involved sending more money. These letters are among the folksiest in the song business, and some of them run to more than five pages of single-spaced typescript. "I'd love to meet you in person, so if you ever get to Chicago, we just must get together for dinner," Slim wrote, in one of them. (One conjures up a nightmare picture of scores of hungry songwriters arriving in a solid phalanx for the promised meal.)

The letter went on to ask the recipient to "please call me Slim."

> I have never felt "above" my fans and co-workers. In my opinion, friendship is the greatest thing in the world.
> It has NO Peer. Just because I am a radio entertainer I've never let it go to my head and I never will. . . .

From this and the many letters that followed, Millie Pilipovic built up a fascinating mental picture of her collaborator. He emerged almost saint-like from the mimeographed pages, as a sincere, if much-put-upon, creative genius, dedicated to helping others but fighting an uphill battle against the vicissitudes of black Fate and those unidentified enemies who bestrewed his path with pitfalls and with gin. Indeed, it was hard for Mrs. Pilipovic to imagine two more disparate personalities than these two men with whom she had become involved by mail: the briskly efficient Mr. Hastings, with his far-flung interests (one could see him sitting, broad-chested, behind his giant, three-phoned desk in Hollywood, pushing buttons, rasping out orders to minions, and dictating, endlessly); and the earnest, God-fearing, embattled cowboy balladeer, pouring out his personal emotional problems to "my wonderful friend," as he called Millie—and whoever else received his mail-order correspondence.

Slim wrote that "a lot of my friends tell me of their struggles and disappointments in songwriting," and then listed his own troubles and disappointments in heart-breaking detail. In another letter (this one a mere four single-spaced pages) he wrote that "I fully realize that many of my friends have been 'let down' by unscrupulous individuals in this business. I get letters from good, honest, hard-working people who tell me of their bad breaks in life. It hurts me. . . ." Then he wrote that "an effort has been made to POISON your mind against me" and went on to explain that "if I WERE a crook, a swindler, a confidence man, a song shark—or whatever I have been called—I would not be sitting in Chicago, Illinois as president of two respected corporations. . . ." Later, in the same letter, he went on to say that "I am going through such a financial and mental strain that I am sure to suffer a nervous breakdown if I don't [take a vacation]." Rest assured, however, Slim added: if any recordings were due he would be sending them shortly.

When I visited Mrs. Pilipovic, in July 1959, six months after she had paid her $82.50, the recordings she had paid for had still not arrived: only another mimeographed letter from Yodelling Slim asking her to "sit tight. You'll hear from me."

Meanwhile, another company, Star-Crest Recordings, had been examining Mrs. Pilipovic's songs. Somewhat to her surprise, the first form letter was a turn-down.

> Returning rejected material is an unpleasant task. . . .
> I am sorry to advise you that our review department found
> the enclosed not acceptable for recording at this time.

This was the first rejection that Millie Pilipovic, budding songwriter, had ever received; was it possible that this was a legitimate firm genuinely interested in making money from songs and not from songwriters?

A week later, a second form letter arrived from Star-Crest.

You have a song that is being considered for recording. Please fill out and return the enclosure as soon as possible. This is all the information I have at this time. I will advise you of any new developments. Good luck.

Cheered by this turn of events, Mrs. Pilipovic complied. In time she received a third form.

At last I am able to send you some good news!
I have received a report from the reviewing department today.
Out of the thousands of songs and poems that have been reviewed over the past months, a relatively small group has been selected for test-recording. Among those picked for the test was "Grief and Sorrow."

Mrs. Pilipovic read on and discovered that she must pay $96.20 for the privilege of having her song put on a record. The last of the scales fell from her eyes. She had paid for her lessons and saw no reason to pay more. She filed the correspondence and held on to her money. She still writes songs for pleasure, but she no longer deals with the sharks of Hollywood.

5

After two years and an expenditure of $281.50, Millie Pilipovic finally learned certain facts about the music business in North America:

About 80,000 songs are copyrighted every year in the United States alone, most of them unpublishable. Thousands of these have melodies written for a fee by a hack writer who takes varying sums for his work. According to Syde Berman, of the Songwriters' Educational Committee, New York, not one of these songs copyrighted over the past twenty years has ever become a near-successful song, let alone a hit.

According to Broadcast Music Inc., "there are probably not more than 150 popular numbers published by reputable publishers every year which make money either for the composer or for the publisher."

It costs from ten to fifteen thousand dollars to exploit a popular song successfully, and often it has cost a great deal more.

No legitimate publisher ever buys a song without music, or charges for the publication of a song, or requires the author to buy copies of the song, or pay for arrangements or in any other way contribute to the publishing of the song. No legitimate publisher solicits for songs by advertising or through the mails; he doesn't have to. No legitimate publisher buys music written for lyrics by paid hacks; these hacks are known to Tin Pan Alley and avoided. No paid-for melody ever crops up on the lists of a legitimate publisher. Nor do legitimate publishers ever buy the lyrics that appear in "vanity" anthologies of the kind published by Eagle Pass.

Yet the newspapers continue to carry stories of rank amateurs who appear to have scored fantastic successes in the music world. How do they get these stories? They get them the same way my paper got its scoop on Millie Pilipovic—from the song sharks themselves, who must, after all, live up to their commitments to promote these paid-for songs.

A short time after I talked to Mrs. Pilipovic, two press releases came in to the city desk of the *Star*. The first was from the Star Crest Recording Company, and was addressed to the Hometown Editor, Local News Department.

We are issuing recording contracts on a song composed by a writer in your town. Any immediate advance publicity or mention you are able to give will be most appreciated by all concerned and should prove an interesting item for your "local news" section.

After listing the name and address of the rural housewife involved, the company added this significant postscript: "Would you please send us a copy of your display rates? We will be happy to keep your company in mind for future advertising needs."

The second item was from my old pen-pal, John White of Nordyke, and it contained the usual capitalizations.

> A GREAT LOCAL EVENT HAS OCCURRED! NORDYKE Music Publishing Co........has the honor and privilege to announce the DISCOVERY of a fine NEW Songwriter, Annie Mable Pettit, 29 Durham Street, Ajax, Ontario, CANADA (Housewife, Mother of nine), creator of "MY MAMMA." The struggles of this NEW songwriter and the circumstances surrounding his [sic] sudden rise to prominence as a result of this song's PUBLICATION are facts which merit the warmest interest and widest publicity. . . .

The letter went on and on and on, but the assistant city editor who picked it up was a wiser man by now. He stopped reading at this point and tossed it in the basket with the rest of the trash.

4

Don't Sell the Product: Sell the Story

Some years ago, a woman to whom I am related by marriage purchased a linen tablecloth at the front door for $37—and I haven't let her hear the last of it.

She bought the cloth partly because she felt sorry for the tiny Irishwoman who sold it to her and partly because she thought she was getting a bargain. The woman told her, with a crack in her voice, that she had just arrived in the New World with few funds and fewer prospects and so must sell her proudest possessions.

"I hate to part with it, I do," she had said, fingering the cloth with real affection. "It's been in the family these many years; but, you see, I've been forced to the point, mum, where I'd rather have bread for my children than fine linen on my table."

A week or two later, a neighbor gave a dinner party. There, proudly displayed on the buffet, was an identical Irish linen tablecloth; even the marks of aging seemed to be in the same places. Several guests at the party remarked on its resemblance to tablecloths they had recently purchased from a sad little Irishwoman at their doors. These revelations helped to cushion the blow when, a few weeks later, all the cloths began to fall to pieces.

I have had, since that time, an understandable curiosity about the linen business, and when one day I learned that an acquaintance had actually been a linen salesman in his salad days, I persuaded him to take me behind the scenes. Here is his story, just as he told it into the tape recorder:

"When you sell linen, you don't sell the item, you sell the story. In almost every big city on this continent there are men who have no business addresses, but who work out of a suitcase. They'll buy a stock of brand-new linens from China, which are reproductions of European linens, and then they'll age them. They soak them in coffee and God knows what (coffee is very good for aging); they rub their feet in them; they do anything they can to make them look old. Then they print up stationery with the Italian royal family's crest on it, say, and around it they'll make up the history of the linen—how it came from royal sources and was passed along to this person and that. They age the stationery, too.

"Then they grease their hair down slick and put on a four-button jacket, short, very European in style, and they affect an accent—Italian or Polish. They go to the biggest hotels and knock at the high-class suites. They say they've just got off the boat and haven't any money, and this linen is the only heirloom they were able to take out of their country. In this way they can sell a piece of linen that cost maybe $30 or $40 in China for as much as $5,000—even more. People have become really wealthy that way, just working out of a suitcase selling linen in hotel rooms.

"Many linen shops—in fact, some of the finer linen shops on Fifth Avenue, New York—work in a very interesting way. They will have linens packed into boxes with a sales slip dated perhaps two months back. If they can't close a deal with a prospective customer, they'll say, suddenly: 'Look, I've got something special for you.'

"By this time they've found out what kind of cloth the customer is interested in. They'll pull it out, all wrapped, with the sales slip inside, and they'll tell a story that a visitor to New York left a substantial deposit, say $200, but never came back to pick up the linen or left any forwarding address. So the store will give the prospect the benefit of the $200 down payment. Believe me, it's very easy to close a sale that way.

"Most linen shops carry linens from China which are much cheaper than European linens. The European work is much finer than the Chinese. A *point venice* cloth that sells for $70 in China will quite often have a price of $2,000 on it in North America. Then it'll go on a half-price sale for $1,000, and, in the end, the store will take what it can bargain for, usually $500 or $600.

"But it's the story they sell, not the item. For instance, *point venice* cloth is entirely hand-stitched. If it were done by Americans or Canadians you couldn't put a price on it: but labor is cheap in China. So a sales story will go like this:

"'Little Chinese girls, when they are five or six, start to learn how to sew on unbleached muslins: when they become more skilled, they work on unbleached cottons, then on grass linen, and later on fine linen. Very few ever grow skilled enough to do *point venice* work. Thus one woman will start a *point venice* cloth; her daughter will continue it; and her daughter will finish it. Because, after all, how many years do you think they have left in their eyes after they go through all these stages? And when you buy a cloth like this, madam, *you put on your table the eyes and souls of three generations of Chinese!'*

"Well, you see, that would leave a customer prostrate. She buys a story like that to put on her table and tell to her guests. However, a Chinese factory has no machines: it has a bunch of people sitting on the floor. And the fact of the matter is that this piece of *point venice* they're talking about can be made overnight. You go into a Chinese linen factory, pick a pattern, order it today, and they'll have it for you by morning, because hundreds of people work on it in sections.

"The phrase 'Handmade in China' means nothing because everything over there is handmade. The Chinese can make a handkerchief that takes a magnifying glass to see the stitches: they're so small you can't see them with the naked eye. The salesman will tell you there are guaranteed to be one million stitches in it.

"A store will take such a handkerchief that might cost $2.50 in China and put it in the window with a great big sign: $50 each. Beside it they'll put some little handmade doilies that cost them seven cents, and they'll mark these three cents each. Now you can imagine the effect that this has on someone's mind. If this doily can sell for three cents at a profit, then the price of $50 on the handkerchief must be fair.

"Now the fact is they don't expect to sell that $50 handkerchief. But people come into the store and ask to see it at close range. The clerk will show it off with trembling hands; and invariably the prospect will say: 'Who in the world would pay $50 for a handkerchief?'

"'Ah,' says the clerk, 'what can you give your loved one for $50? A $50 watch is common. Many women have a $50 dress. But who in the world has a $50 handkerchief? A queen! A princess! So when you give your sweetheart a $50 handkerchief you put her in the class of a queen. And this is how you present it to her'—and he takes out a little jewel box and tenderly folds the handkerchief into it.

"Now he switches his pitch and tries to sell the customer a large piece of linen. And he does his best to close the deal, for say $400, offering to throw in the $50 handkerchief as a gift to the customer's wife or sweetheart. That usually does it. I know because I was in the business. As I told you, it's not the linen you sell, it's the story."

2

It is not only in the linen business that the story is sold rather than the product. Much of the merchandise that is peddled on the doorstep comes wrapped in an elaborate and appealing fantasy. The phrase "door-to-door selling" is eschewed in the jargon of the trade; it is called, rather, "direct selling." Actually, it is perhaps the most indirect form of selling extant, since the householder rarely learns at the outset that the pleasant-looking man standing firmly on the Welcome Mat is in fact a salesman.

A man I know who was looking for a job a couple of years ago saw a classified ad in the paper asking for competent advertising men. He applied for the job and was given a course by an organization called World-Wide Distributors, which sells Queen Anne brand stainless-steel cookware. He was not taught the advertising business, however: he was taught to sell.

The secret, he learned, was to appeal to the avarice and

the vanity of the customer. Reduced to a few capsule sentences, the instructions might go like this:

Tell him he's getting something free. Tell him you desperately need his advice. Tell him you'll let him in on a fantastic bargain. Tell him only a Select Few can qualify for the bargain. Tell him he's one of the Select Few. And don't show all your wares at once. Bring a few items out at the end so he thinks he's getting them thrown in for nothing.

My acquaintance was taught that the best way to get into a house was to pretend to be an advertising man, apparently because all the world trusts an advertising man. He was given cards to distribute offering "A LOVELY GIFT FREE" to those who would "give their opinion" of Queen Anne stainless-steel cookware. *This is an advertising program,* the gift card read. *There is no obligation.*

The salesman's first task was to impress upon the customers that they were members of a tightly exclusive group, chosen to help advertise Queen Anne cookware. I quote directly from the sales talk he was given to memorize:

"Now, as I told you folks when I made this appointment with you, I'm with the Advertising Department of World-Wide Distributors. . . . You see, this product is not on the open market for sale yet, but our company has decided to advertise it through the oldest medium of advertising, which is personal recommendation. . . . In other words, Mrs. Jones, all the money we are spending in advertising we're going to spend right in the homes of folks like yourselves. If you can qualify we'll place this set with you on a special promotion basis. . . .

"You'll say this can't happen. No factory would ever make this kind of offer to us. Well, we are making these offers, Mrs. Jones, but unfortunately you do have to qualify if you want to take advantage of them, because right now we're

placing these sets for just one purpose, and that's advertising. . . .

"Now, it will take me just a few minutes to show you what
we have here . . . but what I'm interested in is your reaction—what you can do for us in the form of advertising: and
when I find out, then I can tell you the offer that the company permits me to make to you. O.K.? Oh, incidentally, due
to the nature of this offer, it's good only on the first call. In
other words, I can't come back. . . . Then it wouldn't be
advertising, would it?"

After the salesman demonstrated the cookware set, his
job was to make the customer believe she was getting a real
bargain. He used what is called a "trial closer." He tried to
get husband and wife to agree separately that they would
like to have the set. The questions were phrased so that a
"yes" answer was relatively easy.

To the wife he said: "If you had the opportunity to have
Queen Anne in your home tonight, Mrs. Jones, can you see
what it would do for you?"

To the husband he said: "Wouldn't you like your wife to
have a set of tools like this in your kitchen?"

This kind of question, especially the latter one, has always
seemed to me to be fiendishly cunning. It is, after all, a
callous husband who can bring himself to say "no" to such a
query, especially in front of a stranger and with his wife
right beside him. If the salesman did encounter resistance at
this point from some unfeeling spouse, he was instructed to
repeat his demonstration. Otherwise he plunged on with his
next question: "Do you think the value of this is more or less
than $500?"

This gave him the chance to scrawl $500 in big letters on
his pad, thereby impressing that magic figure in his prospects' minds. (From this point on, by some curious psycho-

logical alchemy, every lesser figure mentioned appeared to constitute a price slash.)

"You'd probably have to pay $400 or $500 for this downtown," the salesman was taught to say, writing *$400* below the first figure, "or at least [with a laugh] $399.99." And he wrote that figure beneath the other two.

"But on this one-offer call my company has given me permission to give you an introductory offer of only $239.50." (He wrote *$239.50* in very small figures on his pad.) "Isn't that wonderful value?" (*Sadly*) "But you *do* have to qualify." (*Brightly*) "The qualifications are pretty simple, though: all you have to do is talk it up among your neighbors and write the company a letter telling them how you like it." (The highball-lowball technique of Mr. Ringer, the car salesman, described in Chapter 1, is evident here.)

At this point the salesman's instructions were to leap up in excitement and produce a fifty-eight piece set of tableware: "I almost forgot! My company has authorized me to include this free with your set."

(What the customers did not know was that, if they continued to resist, the salesman was prepared to drop the price to $189.50 on the pretext of taking their old cookware as a "trade-in." No salesman likes to do this, however, because it cuts the size of his commission.)

Next the salesman had to go through the delicate maneuver of persuading his prospects to sign a contract. His instructions were to tell them that he had two jobs: one was advertising; the other was to explain how they could "acquire" a set. (He was never to use the taboo word "buy.") There were several easy plans; they could make any kind of payments they chose, no matter how small; they could make any down payment that suited them. It sounded unbelievably simple.

The salesman's next move was to pack up his wares and

then, just as he reached the door, to say, as an afterthought: "Oh, Mrs. Jones, I haven't shown you the best part." Out came an electric skillet: "My company includes one of these with every set of cookware when the full $50 is put down." (*Regretfully*) "But, of course, you didn't put that much down, so you won't be getting it." The next move was to start packing again.

"The whole idea was to make them beholden to you—to make them think you were doing them a real favor," my acquaintance explained.

If the couple already owned an electric skillet, the salesman had an alternative gift in his kit, usually a carving set. He was instructed to show this anyway, because he needed it the next time he opened the door to leave.

For it was his final task to pop back once more, crying: "Say! There *is* a way in which you can get this magnificent carving set! My company will also include this in the deal if you'd like to make it a cash sale!" (A cash sale meant an additional $10 commission for the salesman.)

In this way, couple after couple awoke to the bewildering truth that, as a result of an hour spent with an "advertising man," they had laid out $239.50 in cash and were loaded down with a small mountain of cookware, tableware, carving utensils, and electrical equipment. How many people entering the kitchen-supply department of a retail store ever spend that amount in one shopping spree?

This basic technique has been employed, with variations, on thousands of doorways and in thousands of living rooms by salesmen who pretend to be taking a survey on behalf of their company's advertising department. It has been honed to a fine polish in the encyclopaedia field, as a study of the direct-selling techniques of P. F. Collier and Sons, publishers of Collier's Encyclopaedia, shows.

The young students who answered an ad for COLLEGE

MEN (*We have summer jobs for you; $90 a week guaran-teed*) were not told they were to be salesmen either. Indeed, it took them some time to discover who they were working for or what it was all about.

"I made an appointment and sat in a lecture for fifteen minutes and I still had no idea what was going on," one of them told me. "I'd ask: 'Who am I going to be working for? What am I going to be doing?' and they'd find ways of evading the question. It was like one of those movies about how spies were picked in wartime by British Army Intelligence."

I asked a young Notre Dame graduate named Tim Ryan to answer the ad and to hang on grimly until he cracked the mystery. Ryan made a telephone appointment, and the following day he and five other applicants were ushered into a small office and lectured for more than a quarter of an hour on the advantages of give-away sales programs. The experiences of Gleem toothpaste and Salem cigarettes were mentioned, and at first Ryan thought he would be working for one of these firms. Then the applicants were asked whether they would be able to work evenings and Saturdays. Three said they could not and were ushered out, as baffled as my original informant. Ryan and two others stayed on and were rewarded by the revelation that they would take part in a promotional campaign to "place" sets of Collier's Encyclopaedia in "carefully selected homes." They would get $49 for every set they placed. Some men, they were told, placed as many as three or four sets a night. Nothing was said about selling anything. Ryan figured, correctly, that the opening lecture had been a form of brainwashing calculated to convince all the young men that they really were advertising executives and not salesmen.

Of this they were to be swiftly disabused. The following afternoon a carload of applicants, including Tim Ryan, were driven to a suburban area and dumped out. Each was in the company of an old professional who was to demonstrate the artifice of door-to-door selling, and each was armed with several documents: a "door opener" spiel, which he was to memorize word for word; a long and involved sales pitch, complete with instructions showing where to laugh; and some handsome literature about the encyclopaedia and other books. Nothing more was said about carefully selected homes. Indeed, the printed instructions read: *Don't pass up a house!* The job of these salesmen was to knock on every door in the block and try to get inside. Ryan and his companion got inside two out of fifteen but sold no books. Nothing more was said about the guaranteed salary either, so Ryan quit, but not before he took down the details of Collier's sales pitch, which was particularly elaborate, occupying eleven pages of closely typed foolscap. It is worth examining in some detail:

The "door opener" is especially hard to resist unless you are that hated personality which the company refers to as a "hard-head" ("Don't waste time on hard-heads at the door," salesmen are advised:)

"Hi, I wonder if you could give me some information? I am doing some advertising work in the neighborhood this afternoon for the Collier company. Now, Collier is putting on the market a brand-new three-million-dollar program. It is new to us, new to the public, and completely out of the magazine field. In each area where the program will be sold, the company, at this time, is interviewing several families to get local critical comment. For any help I receive, Collier is in a position to pay for it. So there's a couple of questions I'd like to ask you folks. Do you mind?"

Under the pretext, then, of getting critical comments (and supposedly paying for them), the salesman enters the house, gets both husband and wife together, and gives the impression that Collier's, having left the magazine field, is launching a new book-publishing business. These various books will shortly be sold in the stores, he explains, but first the company is testing them out on a few selected families, to get "local comment and criticism."

The salesman first introduces the Collier Junior Classics, the company's "first attempt to go into the literary field." He explains that this is a collection of the world's greatest classical stories which, after it is introduced, will retail for slightly more than ten cents per story—or $79.50 for a complete set.

Then the salesman introduces the *pièce de resistance,* which is the Collier's Encyclopaedia. He is careful not to call it an encyclopaedia at the beginning, since this, like "magazine," "subscription," "buy," and "sell," is not an Okay Word. He calls it a "reference library," and he says it is the first brand-new major reference library to be published in more than thirty-five years. Throughout the sales pitch the inference is always that the program is a brand-new one; that a test is being made; that within a very short time this reference library will be sold in the normal way through retail channels. (Actually, Collier's Encyclopaedia, available since 1950 and conceived in 1946, is still not being sold through retail channels.)

The next move is to convince the family that it will receive both the reference library and the children's encyclopaedia absolutely free in return for helping the Collier company. This not inconsiderable feat is achieved in this manner:

"I think you folks can see that Collier is going into this very extensively. In introducing it for the first time into a large metropolitan area like Toronto, we have found there is one big reaction we have to overcome. The first thing that nine out of ten families ask is, 'Has anyone in the neighborhood bought one yet?' . . . What Jack has, John is inclined to trust. . . .

". . . Collier, realizing the importance of this attitude and
the effect it has on sales potential, at this time is dividing the
area into square sections. We are calling on several families
in each section and with a couple of qualified families placing
this new library as a premium in return for permission to
use their names as local owners. . . ."

The name is not an endorsement, the salesman hastens to
assure his prospects. It is merely a statement of ownership.
It is, like a library list, used only to reassure the neighbors
that some respected people own the set, when the actual
sales campaign begins in a year or so.

I can remember, years ago, shortly after my wife and I
were married, a crisp young man arriving at our door to explain that we had been especially selected to receive an encyclopaedia at bargain rates. I did not buy that particular
encyclopaedia, but I do confess to a feeling of pride in being among the chosen. Indeed, I felt rather badly that lack
of funds made it impossible for me to help out the young
advertising man who was so flattering to us both. Why, he
had said, the fact that *we* had an encyclopaedia in our
apartment would make an enormous impression on the
neighborhood. That was why his company was prepared to
place one in our home at bargain rates.

Collier's pitch, however, is cleverer since it doesn't mention
a bargain price. In this case the prospects are told the encyclopaedia is absolutely free!

"If it were possible for the Collier company, within the
next ten days or two weeks, to ship you this new program—
that is, both libraries, parcel post, prepaid, yours to keep as
an advertising premium without the normal costs involved—
would you be willing to do two things for Collier's in return?"

The salesman has reached that key point in all direct-sales
pitches known as "the qualifying question." In sales parlance, a prospect "qualifies," not by reason of social prestige,

wealth, or personal integrity, but simply by answering one or two questions in the affirmative. These questions are phrased in such a way that the prospect himself seems to be asking the salesman to supply him with the product. The stratagem is known as "getting a commitment" from the prospect, and it has immense psychological value, akin to that dramatic moment in revival meetings when a nonbeliever, carried away by the emotion of the moment, commits himself to a Christian life. The very phrasing has an evangelical ring. More often than not the qualifying questions are preceded by the words: "Do you honestly and sincerely believe . . . ?" It reminds one a bit of a catechism learned in Confirmation class.

The salesman outlines the two things that the customers are to be asked to do in order to get all these free books. One has already been mentioned—they must allow their names to be used as owners. The second is more subtle and more significant:

"Would you appreciate and respect the library and the idea behind it enough to keep it up to date if Collier's sent it to you?" (After all, the salesman explains, the company does not want it to be a dust gatherer.)

"Now my job is to explain what we mean by keeping it up to date . . . but first I am supposed to ask you two questions:

"If everything else were agreeable, would you have any possible objection to your name appearing on this owners' register?"

He waits for an answer and then proceeds:

"Do you honestly and sincerely believe that the library would be valuable in your home, both now as well as in the years to come?" Collier salesmen are warned that the customers must "qualify strongly" before they can proceed.

The catechism having been completed, the salesman then

explains that, once a year, the Collier company publishes a Year Book in order to keep its encyclopaedia up to date. In addition it has a research bureau which encyclopaedia owners can use to answer questions. He explains both these bonus features in some detail. Then he points out that the encyclopaedia is nationally advertised at $389. (He does not say that it rarely sells at that price: A recent inquiry placed the cash price at $245.50.)

At this point the salesman moves in swiftly to close the deal. Within the next ten days to two weeks, he explains, "the Collier company would like to ship you folks the complete ten-volume set of the Collier Junior Classics, and the complete twenty-volume set of the brand new Collier's Encyclopaedia bound in DuPont Fabricoid. Now, both these libraries would be shipped parcel post, prepaid, yours to keep as premiums at no cost now or ever."

He asks only two things. First, the use of the name, and second, that they keep the library up to date by means of a "revision service," which consists of the Year Book and the research bureau. "To send this combined service to a family costs the Collier company, in royalties and printings, just $27.95 a year. Under this promotional plan, that is absolutely all they ask for the entire program. The only obligation on it to Collier would be moral. . . ."

Before the prospects can do the necessary arithmetic, the salesman has rattled on. (*No pause here*, his directions read, *go directly to next sentence.*) He recapitulates some of his sales pitch in order to prepare them for another financial shock. Then he says:

"Well, you folks have taken this very calmly. Most people couldn't believe that there wasn't a catch connected with it."

Then he explains that when the retail program goes into effect "next year" the Year Book by itself will sell for $16.50. (It will, too, if anybody insists on paying that much for it;

few do.) This means that during the next ten years, the actual value of the material sent out will come to around $900. But the qualified families will pay only $27.95 a year. Because families move about a lot, "binding, shipping, and customs" of the Year Book are being handled separately to avoid confusion. Binding, shipping, and customs charges will come to an additional $4.95 a year, paid on the delivery of the Year Book each April.

Now the salesman moves into his final, closing argument. The only thing that Collier asks is that any family who wishes to participate in this program does not take ten years to handle it—because the costs of bookkeeping would be enormous. "So we set up a plan for the use of families . . ."

He produces a standard non-cancellable conditional sales contract, though he does not call it that. He calls it "a written guarantee." This irrevocably commits the family to monthly payments over a two-year period. The salesman explains this in a curious way:

"This is your copy of the guarantee. . . . I've dated it here, signed it here, and receipted you here and here for the first payment that must accompany the order. Also I have set up your next payment for the fourteenth. Also, you have probably read that this is not subject to any written or verbal cancellation or alteration, nor is it affected by an agreement not stated herein. This is for the family's protection and the company's—it means that no matter what the company's cost would rise to, you folks could never be billed any more than stated herein."

It also means that, once the contract is signed, the family cannot wriggle out of it. They must make those payments, totaling $279.50, plus $49.50 for Year Books, or face court action and garnishee proceedings; and any promises the salesman may have made will have no legal meaning.

Three years after Tim Ryan learned how to sell encyclopaedias, the identical techniques (differing only in degree and detail from those of several other encyclopaedia-sales forces) were still being used in my neighborhood by Collier.

Householders were told the same story: that this was a new work of reference; that the company was trying it out by placing it in the hands of a few selected people for advertising purposes; that very shortly it would be sold from retail outlets; that it was absolutely free and all the lucky people had to do was to keep it up to date.

The 1962 offer varied slightly from the 1959 offer in that a Bible and bookcase were included with the Junior Classics. The price had increased to $369.50.

This turned out to be the exact price quoted to anyone who offered to buy for cash directly from the company. Without Bible, bookcase, or Junior Classics, the price was $245.50, with the Year Books at $3.95 apiece, and the research service supplied at no extra charge. But the especially selected families were not told that.

3

One evening in the fall of 1959, Mrs. Donald Bant, a good-looking former model, newly arrived from England, received a telephone call at her home in Scarborough, a middle-class suburb of Toronto.

"Isn't this a beautiful evening, Mrs. Bant," said the cheerful voice, and Mrs. Bant had no idea he was reading from a script or that she was being sold a story.

"I called you this evening to ask your help with a couple of questions," the man on the phone said, "but first I'd better tell you whom I am with.

"This is the research division of International Health Products. We are the people who are introducing the fabulous new Health Maid electric servant—an entirely new concept in modern living. This revolutionary new all-purpose kitchen machine is not yet available to the public, Mrs. Bant. We are conducting this research program as part of our educational program in order to show some of the wonders of tomorrow, and how the average Canadian family can have better nutrition and health from their food."

If Mrs. Bant had not been a newcomer to these shores, she would, in all likelihood, have hung up the phone at this point. Instead, she found herself nodding in agreement when the voice went on to say: "You *are* interested in better nutrition and health for your family if it's possible to get it, aren't you, Mrs. Bant? Most people who *think* are!

"Since you are interested in nutrition and health, Mrs. Bant, I would like to arrange your appointment to see this wonderful work and time saver and have you qualify for a chance to win one of these fabulous electric servants. In return, Mrs. Bant, all we ask is that after seeing this amazing machine you will fill out a simple questionnaire giving your honest opinions about it—that's not asking too much, is it?"

Mrs. Bant had been ill for some time. Her husband was out of work. Both were heavily committed to payments for household goods. She told the man she could not afford to buy anything. He assured her he was not selling anything; he was merely asking for opinions.

"This preview that you'll be seeing is solely for research purposes, Mrs. Bant," he said. "We are not selling anything. . . . Health is something you can't *sell*—but must be *earned*, so we are only interested in those people who have a desire to do something for themselves."

Mrs. Bant said she didn't have much time.

"Well, Mrs. Bant," said the man on the phone, "we only

have two things in this life to spend—time and money, and if both of these things are not spent wisely, we can neither have health nor anything else for long—isn't that true?" He didn't wait for Mrs. Bant to say whether it was true or not, but plunged on: "For that reason, Mrs. Bant, it is really in *your* interest to take a few minutes of your valuable time to see what we have—we won't try to sell you anything—that I promise."

Mrs. Bant succumbed, and presently, a man named Mr. McGregor arrived at her door. Mr. McGregor said that he was deeply and sincerely interested in the health of the nation. He had a letter from his company, whose office was identified as the Eglinton Health Centre. He read from the letter, which bemoaned the fact that "here we are living in a land of plenty with literally thousands of people suffering from malnutrition—the open door through which many other crippling diseases enter to destroy our health and rob us of our happiness." He talked knowingly about recent surveys which proved that the majority of school children were not properly nourished, because they ate meager breakfasts. All this, he said, could be prevented by a few simple adjustments in eating habits.

Mr. McGregor stressed the importance of milk in diet, explaining that it was the greatest nutritional source of calcium and protein—something most children were not getting in sufficient quantity. He was gathering opinions, he said, on a new form of powdered milk. He brought a package of the milk powder into the house, and also a machine, which he said was necessary to mix the milk.

Mrs. Bant again explained that she could not afford to buy anything, but Mr. McGregor kept insisting he wasn't selling anything. He explained that the milk he was demonstrating was ten times better than milk available in the stores because of the process used to mix it. He demonstrated the marvelous machine which liquefied, blended, ground, whipped, mixed, pureed, and pulverized not only milk powder, but also vegetables, fruit, salad dressing, sauces, nuts, meats, cheese, cream, egg whites, batter, sherbet, baby food, and dried peas. It was the world's most sensible kitchen aid, said the knowledgeable Mr. McGregor.

Mrs. Bant said she could not afford to buy one. Mr. McGregor again explained firmly that the machine was not for sale. He would like her to fill out his questionnaire; that was all.

Mr. McGregor returned to the subject of milk as an important nutritional aid, and its cost to an average family. With two children, he said, Mrs. Bant must be paying $16 a month for milk; if she was not spending that much, he said, then her children weren't getting enough calories. And Mr. McGregor, who wasn't selling anything, reeled off some figures to prove his point.

"Why," said Mr. McGregor, "you're spending $2,000 a decade on milk, and all you've got to show for it is a lot of empty milk bottles.

"If I were to hold in my left hand all the empty milk bottles you wash in a month and in my right hand I hold the same amount of milk, plus this wonderful machine, which hand would you think was the greater value?"

Mrs. Bant was bewildered. She found herself saying the right hand. On hearing that, Mr. McGregor said he wanted to ask her a very special question:

"If I could do something very special for you, would you do something very special for me in return?"

It is a hard question to say "no" to. Mrs. Bant found herself nodding.

"It's obvious from your answer that you appreciate the importance of your family's health and realize it's something that must have proper care, if you are to maintain it. Right?

Frankly, there just aren't enough people who appreciate this fact, but in introducing new health products, when we do find a family such as yours, we have something to offer them. . . . Now, if we are able to offer you one of these wonderful units as part of this program, without disturbing your weekly budget a penny, would you be interested?"

Mrs. Bant said that she supposed she would be.

Mr. McGregor then explained that, because of her interest in her family's health, his company was prepared to supply her with powdered milk; she would pay no more for it than she was paying for ordinary milk for her family. Furthermore, the company would let her have the machine free —if she would promise to use it.

Mrs. Bant's conscience had been stirred by all the talk of poor nutrition; and the way the salesman put it, she did not see how she could lose. She said she would like to have time to think it over, but Mr. McGregor said that was impossible; the offer was only good for the one evening.

Mrs. Bant asked what would happen if her children didn't like the milk. Mr. McGregor replied that his company would take the machine back immediately. He had a form for her to sign, he said; it was merely routine, but their lawyers insisted that they use it. Mrs. Bant, who thought she was getting a real bargain, signed. She signed up for fifteen pounds of powdered skim milk a month and promised to make nineteen payments of $16 each, together with a down payment of another $16. In other words, she committed herself to a debt of $320. The form she signed was a promissory note.

The next day Mrs. Bant discovered that one of her children, who had a weak stomach, could not take the milk preparation. She also discovered that powdered milk, when bought at a grocery store, would cost her about $6 a month. She phoned International Health Products and tried to reach the salesman. He wasn't in. She left a message for him to call. He didn't call. When, after considerable difficulty, she finally reached him, he told her she must make her child drink the milk.

She called the manager of International Health Products and asked him to take the milk and the machine back. She said she was willing to forgo the down payment, but wanted neither the milk nor the machine. The manager told her that she had signed a promissory note and was liable for more than $300. She could pay or go to court, he said. He advised her to get a loan somewhere.

Mrs. Bant said that in England ethical companies took things back if the purchaser wasn't satisfied.

"Well, you're not in England now," the manager said. "Things are done differently in Canada. Over here you don't believe anything unless it's written down and signed." She had signed a note, he explained; she would have to pay.

Mrs. Bant's husband took the machine back personally. A company representative refused to accept it. It was, he insisted, a second-hand machine now. He refused to give Mr. Bant a receipt for it, and so Mr. Bant took the machine home again.

When Mrs. Bant persisted in phoning again and again, the company changed its tactics. It offered to send her half the amount of milk contracted for and to reduce her payments to $13.50 a month; then it offered to suspend all milk-powder shipments if she would make payments of $11 a month for the machine. But she must pay for the machine, the manager said, or she would be taken to court. There was no further talk about the nutritional importance of milk, and it dawned on Mrs. Bant that it was the machine and not the milk the salesman was really peddling. At $11 a month, she was being charged about $220 for a combination blender, mixer, and grinder similar to those which retailed in department stores for less than $80.

Mrs. Bant made a final telephone call to International Health Products and was connected with a Mr. Keene. I listened to the conversation on an extension, and it was a tough one. Mr. Keene told Mrs. Bant flatly that "any arrangements the salesman makes won't stand up"; that "a man's word is something that's not accepted over here in Canada"; that Mrs. Bant had signed a promissory note, "which in actual fact has nothing to do with the merchandise, it's a loan"; that she was leaving herself wide open to court action, which would result in a garnishee of her wages; that the court would order her employer to turn one third of what she earned over to International Health Products; and that, "if you're out of work, we'll just watch you until you get a job—there are organizations which will track you down."

The story, of course, has no end. That conversation, or one very like it, is being repeated over and over again in every large city on the continent. Housewives are still answering doorbells and signing those innocent little forms that have so many teeth in them. And some of them are waiting to be sued.

4

Robert Fulford, a book and art critic who is a colleague of mine and not a typical mooch at all, was at home working on a book review one morning in October 1960 when a fifteen-year-old boy knocked on his door.

"The boy surprised me by being rather like myself at that age," Bob told me, in recounting the story later. "As soon as I opened the door, he began lying to me in a shy and charming way. He knew just how to smile and show boyish modesty."

Bob recalled that when he was that age he also knew how to lie. Later he stopped because the adults he admired made it plain to him that it was unmanly. But here was a boy who had been taught by men he admired that lying was the quick way to a sale.

The fairy tale that this youth was given to use was designed to appeal not to the avarice or the vanity of the subject but merely to his sense of charity. I obtained a copy of a very similar one, mimeographed for mass distribution to the small army of boys who are trained to lure long-term subscriptions out of motherly housewives. The comments in italics were supplied me by another self-assured teen-ager who had been taught the techniques of the sympathy sell.

"It's awful what they are teaching kids these days," this cool young man said to me. "The whole training process we went through was designed to convince us that methods don't matter as long as you make a sale. If you can make a dollar, the gimmicks you use are supposed to be okay. The whole dirty, rotten business ought to be exposed."

"Tell me about it," I suggested, "and maybe I can expose it."

He gave me a shrewd look. "Hold on a minute," he said. "What's it worth to you? I got to get something out of it, you know."

It was worth a modest sum, and when the sum was paid, the socially conscious youth agreed to expose the whole dirty rotten business on my recording machine. Here is the way he was taught to sell, with his own comments to me in italics:

Hello, there: You're Mrs. Jones? Gee, I hope I didn't take you away from anything. My name's John Doe and I just dropped by to get your approval on the boys' tour of Europe. (*You never ever mention that you're selling magazines. Nobody wants magazines. They absolutely don't want them.*

They'll often open the door and say: "If you're selling maga-
zines, I don't want any." But they like the idea of a kid get-
ting an education through a tour of Europe, so when you
say this they always relax.)

I guess you've heard all about it, haven't you? You
haven't? Gee, I guess we're not as famous as I thought. I'll
have to explain it to you. Mind if I step in? I'll just show you
how it works. You see, each name on my pad counts for me as
an approval, and when I get 200 of these approvals I qualify
for the tour. (*When you start out you just invent the names*
on your pad. But then you get real names. If people don't
buy magazines you say: "I'll just take your name to show I
called," and you write it down. As soon as people see their
neighbors' names on your pad they feel at ease.)

Now, that's a complete tour of England, Ireland, Scot-
land and Wales, and part of the continent, and that's certainly worth working for, isn't it? (*Actually, we work on a*
straight commission of 45 per cent. There are two contests a
year and if you win both of them you're supposed to get the
tour; I don't know if anybody has ever got it.) Have you ever
done much traveling yourself? You haven't! Gee, I guess
you're like my mother, the only traveling she ever does is
around the kitchen, with a broom. (*This arouses sympathy.*)
Do you know Mrs. Smith down the street? (*Pick someone*
she's heard of but doesn't actually know.) Well, she really
had me laughing. She said, John, if all it takes is my name
and eight cents a month to send you over to England, you
can count me in twice. But there's one little catch—if you do
win the tour you'll have to take me along with you. Of course,
she was only fooling, but she's a real nice lady, isn't she?
(*She never said anything of the sort.*)

Oh, I'm sure you can afford eight cents a month, too, can't
you, along with the rest of your neighbors? Fine, thanks very
much. I certainly appreciate this. How do you spell your last

name, and your first initial is ——? I'll leave you a ballot here. It shows you approved of the tour. (*The "ballot" is actually a receipt for magazines the customer still doesn't know she's going to buy. Yet she's already reaching for it.*) And this is the journal we've arranged to send around to the home. (*You never, never use the word "magazine"; that's a dead word. You say "journal" and you sort of make it sound like the boys are putting it out themselves.*)

It's *Liberty* and it's the best we could find and we're allowed to send it out in small groups of copies. (*You size up the customer and fit the magazine to him:* Liberty *or* Saturday Night *for men:* Maclean's *or* Chatelaine *for women. You never mention the content of the publication. If you sold on anything but sympathy you'd be out of business. No matter what the magazine costs—*Liberty's *a dime,* Chatelaine *fifteen cents—the price is always eight cents.*)

I get my points according to the number of copies you try. (*The words "buy" and "sell" are never used; it's always "try"!*) Like, 300 copies gives me 15 points; 200, ten; 100, four; 75, two; and 50 copies being a small one gives me one point in the contest. Now the idea of points here is if one person should try more copies than another, it's only right it should count more for me, and it's also a more efficient way to determine the winner of the contest. So most of your neighbors have been saying, since they can get the journal so cheap from me, why not get it for a good long term and make sure I do win the tour. So they have been trying the 200 and 100 copies.

(*If you buy 200 copies it means you've signed up to take* Liberty *for 16 years. One Japanese lady was already signed up with* Liberty *until 1979; I signed her for 300 more copies. That's 24 more years on paper, but when you buy in large quantities it's more. In her case it was actually 47 years, which means she was signed up with* Liberty *until the year 2026.*)

You'd never guess what happened to me today. I had two ladies try the 300 copies and give me fifteen points each. I guess this is my lucky day today. (*Nobody that I know has ever signed two people up for 300 copies in one day.*) I make you the third? (*Pause*) Or is that too many? That's too many. Oh, well, we'll just count you in for a small one, say 100 copies. (*This "small" one is eight years, but after the mention of 300, it seems small.*) And if you ever send it to anyone as a gift or write the company for more copies, you be sure to mention my name, as it may count a little extra for me later on. Now, you will be sure to mention my name, won't you? (*The idea is to keep them saying "yes"; they're buying without knowing it.*)

Well, that was 100 copies you wanted, wasn't it? Like, you are giving me four points in the contest. Are you good at mathematics, or are you like me, do you need a paper and pencil? Well, that's 100 copies at eight cents a copy. That works out to an even $8. (*This is the first mention of any sum over eight cents.*) And here's your receipt. (*She hasn't yet given you the money, but she automatically takes it.*) It shows you have paid me today. I hope you haven't got a twenty for me to change—I'm a little short of change today. (*As you say this, you put everything away. That way there's less chance of losing the order. You're all finished, see? And the only thing left for her is to give you the money.*)

Who lives next door? I'll go and call on her next. (*Most of the time they really don't know what's going on. You try to get cash, but if they give you a check you go right down to the bank and certify it. Otherwise hubby comes home and stops payment. The way they look at it, they're not paying money to a magazine company at all; they're sponsoring a tour to Europe to help out a boy. Some of the boys are twenty-six years old. Your age doesn't matter as long as you look young and can make the sales talk sound sincere.*)

Sincerity here is the key word. And sincerity is taught with cold precision, down to the last memorized chuckle and the final prefabricated homily, to these miniature adults who are hired by the big subscription agencies and provided with a story that sells.

Bob Fulford told me that when he heard such a boy, chattering away to him, parrot-fashion, he began to think about the implications of a society where it is possible for a respectable man to earn a living corrupting children, and get away with it, not just legally but also morally and socially.

"Here is a boy," thought Bob, "who has been taught to use the evil in himself—the very thing the schoolbooks preach against—in order to make money. Somewhere, some solid citizens in the publishing business have contrived to teach this kid that lying is profitable. At the most difficult and the most impressionistic and the most terrifying stage in life, he is being initiated into a world where, as far as he can see, lies are more profitable than truth."

The boy finished his story and Bob declined the magazines and the boy trotted down the steps and up to the neighbor's doorstep and began his fairy tale all over again and Bob went back to his work feeling more than a little sad.

5

How to Win Sales and Lose Friends

For seven years the Reverend Robert K. Harris had been pastor at a small country church at Colborne in southeastern Ontario. His policy was to live by faith as far as finances went. His church had told him that he could have a small salary each week if enough money turned up in the collection plate. If not, he must make do with what there was. He made do; at no time did his income exceed $2,500 a year.

It was a life of bare subsistence, nourished by the pastor's fierce faith that the Lord would supply his needs; yet there were times when that faith came close to wavering. He had a wife and two children to support, and when a new baby arrived, an avalanche of bills descended on him. At about the same time, one of the families in his pastorate left, and this loss of support in a tiny community contributed to the blow. Mr. Harris confesses to a feeling of panic; then, once again, he and his wife decided to put their trust in the Lord: "Like Job of old we cried, 'Though He slay us, yet will we trust Him!' "

Two days after this decision, there appeared in the Harrises' mailbox a letter which seemed to come as an answer to a prayer. It was penned by a fellow minister who explained that he had recently talked with a man who had been highly recommended to him by reputable members of his congregation. This man had told him of something new and unique, which had already begun to benefit him and his wife financially and in other ways. The minister went on to say that he had taken the liberty of giving this man the Harrises' name and address. When he came to call, they should both listen attentively to everything he had to say. The letter added that there was nothing to sell and no financial outlay required. There was a postscript in which the reverend gentleman wrote that he was sorry to be so vague, but that he had investigated the situation thoroughly and found it to be bona fide.

To Mr. and Mrs. Harris, this news seemed almost too good to be true. Was it a hoax? Hardly. Both knew the minister in question; Mr. Harris had worked with him. He was an honest man incapable of guile. Besides, as he said, he had investigated the reputability of the scheme. As Mr. Harris later put it: "If I couldn't trust a fellow minister, I couldn't trust anyone."

Both men taught religious education at the local public school, and the following day they met in the hall.

"What's it all about?" Mr. Harris asked.

"If you got my letter, just be patient and you'll find out," replied his colleague. Beyond that he would say no more. The suspense was tantalizing.

The following day Mr. Harris received a call from a Mrs. McLean, who asked if he had received the letter. Mrs. McLean told him that her company's representative would be in the area that afternoon. She made an appointment for 2 p.m.

It was a busy time for Mr. Harris. There was a special Holy Week meeting at an interdenominational church in the neighboring town of Aylmer. Still, thought he: "If this is God's way of meeting our need, I had better spare this man an hour."

As he had been told by his fellow minister to listen carefully, Mr. Harris and his wife gave the man who arrived on their doorstep their undivided attention, concentrating on everything he said. There followed an hour-long demonstration, in the Harrises' kitchen, of a water-conditioning unit designed to turn hard water into soft water, to save on soap, to clean clothes and dishes more efficiently, and to benefit the human body through the removal of "injurious chemicals," which the stranger said might cause kidney stones and gall-bladder trouble.

Following the demonstration, the Harrises and their visitor returned to the living room. Here the couple learned that the water-conditioning firm wanted them to supply it with a list of names of friends and acquaintances whom its representatives could contact for similar demonstrations. These could not be names copied from the telephone directory; they must be actual relatives or friends. Mr. Harris was told that, besides supplying the company with the list of names, he must be prepared to send a letter to each one exactly like the one he had received from his colleague in the ministry.

It was just like belonging to a club, the Harrises were told; surely if such an association were going to benefit them, they would want their friends to share it! Then the stranger explained in detail exactly how things worked.

The Harrises would receive $25 for every person to whom

they wrote, provided that person allowed a demonstration and then "joined up" in the club. Then, for every name that these new members supplied who also joined, the Harrises would receive an additional $25. This amounted to a week's income for Mr. and Mrs. Harris. In addition, for the name of a friend who permitted a demonstration but did not join, they would receive five dollars. This arrangement was good for three years, and the stranger with the water conditioner produced a written guarantee of profit sharing.

There was only one strict rule, the man said: After their friends had been advised of the wonderful opportunity in store for them, the Harrises must not give out any further information—*no matter what kind of questions they were asked.* The company representative, after all, could explain the matter far more effectively and accurately than anybody else.

Mr. Harris agreed with enthusiasm. How could they lose? he asked himself. Even as he spoke, a list of ministerial friends in similar straitened circumstances flashed through his mind. They also could use some ready cash.

The visitor next went on to explain that, in order to join the club, it would be necessary for the couple to sign a contract permitting the company to attach a conditioning unit to the water supply. Mr. Harris replied that that would be impossible since they did not own the house and their widowed landlady lived in a small apartment at the rear. "Oh," said the stranger, "that's no problem, really; you'll actually be doing her a service, bringing her the wonderful physical benefits of soft water. And, of course, if you move, the company will move the unit for you free of charge." Thus were the Harrises' fears set at rest.

Then, to the Harrises' surprise and delight, they were given a generous supply of soap chips, together with hand and face soap and a hundred-pound bag of salt to use in the water softener.

Their visitor's next remark, however, came as something of a shock. They had been told specifically that there was to be no financial outlay on their part. Now, Mr. Harris learned that the contract called for him to pay $389 for the unit, plus $30 for installation, plus $175 in carrying charges over a three-year period—a total of $594.

Of course, the water-conditioner man pointed out, the carrying charges would be decreased if the unit were paid off in less time. With the names the Harrises would supply, it shouldn't take any time at all, he said. Mr. Harris tried to read the contract, but as he did this his visitor began to re-cite a list of members, many of whom were familiar to him, who, the visitor said, had already paid off their units and made as much as $1,000 the first year. Everything seemed fairly clear to Mr. Harris. How could he lose, since the idea was brand new in his area and he was among the first to be approached?

Mr. Harris made it clear that his financial circumstances were meager and that, if he did not get a response to his list of names, he would not be able to meet the payments; but his visitor laughed and assured him that this was impossible. He said he would guarantee that out of every ten names they would get $25 from at least seven. Besides, he added, the company did not want any bad publicity. If Mr. Harris could not pay, his firm would remove the unit and that would be that. "Why," he said, "it's quite likely that the company will just leave this unit here out of good will and you'll never hear from them again."

He seemed, as Mr. Harris later put it, a "straight-forward sort of person." The minister saw no reason not to sign the document. Besides, the appointment he had been told would run one hour had taken two hours and a half, and he could ill afford to take any more time over it. The Harrises signed the contract and gave their visitor ten names and addresses. Mr. Harris's instructions were to make ten copies of the letter he had received, put them into individual sealed envelopes bearing his return address, and then place them in a large envelope provided by the company and bearing the address of their regional office. He was assured that these names would not be processed for at least seven days in order to allow time to be sure that he was satisfied with the deal.

Promptly the following morning the water-conditioning unit was installed, and the Reverend Mr. Harris faithfully copied out his letters so that they would look like personal letters to his friends. The following day he left for Aylmer, Ontario, for the Holy Week ceremonies. He spent the weekend in services, but on Monday he visited a young minister friend and his wife in nearby St. Thomas. These people were very close to the Harrises; they shared both their blessings and their problems; it was natural that they should gingerly break the news of a great investment they had made. The young minister rose and took Mr. Harris out to his shed. To the latter's dismay and shock the surprise he had to reveal was a water conditioner.

How could this be? Mr. Harris asked himself. *The whole scheme is supposed to be new and unique. How could they get to hear about it?*

When the two men began to compare notes, they discovered that, although each had dealt with a different company, the details were identical. Mr. Harris's colleague had had his unit for four months, and now he began to explain the heartache it had caused him. In all that time he had not had one response to any of the names he had sent in. Either his friends already had bought water conditioners under similar circumstances or they were not interested.

This young couple's financial state was similar to the Harrises'. They had not been able to meet their payments. The company who made or sold the water conditioners had sold the contract to a finance company. They had, apparently, signed permission for this at the time of the sale. The finance company was demanding its money under the threat of a lawsuit. They had had years of struggle, the husband driving a school bus between ministerial duties, to make ends meet, the wife teaching in a small country school. Finally they had managed to make a down payment on a bungalow. Now they were threatened with its loss.

The Reverend Mr. Harris was horrified at this story. All that night he could not sleep. "I was a gospel minister, and because I was, many people had confidence in me to help them," he explained later. "Now for a measly $25 I was selling that confidence down the river."

He knew what he must do. The following morning he called the company's regional office and tried to reach the salesman. He had no luck—nor was he ever able to reach him. But he did talk to the Mrs. McLean who had first called him. He asked her to destroy the ten letters he had sent in. Mrs. McLean replied that the letters had already been mailed. Wearily, Mr. Harris sat down and wrote follow-up letters to each of these people to tell them under no circumstances to allow the visitor he had recommended to enter their home unless they were interested in paying more than $400 for a water softener.

Meanwhile the water at the Harris home had assumed a briny taste which made it all but undrinkable. In vain Mr. Harris asked the regional manager to take the machine away. He was told firmly that he had signed a contract and was liable for payments. No serviceman arrived and the phone calls to the regional office only produced sharp answers. To make matters worse, Mr. Harris opened a mail-order catalogue and saw a machine that seemed to be identical listed at $199.

Mr. Harris disconnected the water softener and went back to old-fashioned hard water. Presently a process server arrived and handed his wife a document. The finance company, to which the water-conditioning company had sold his contract, was suing the Harrises for $594 plus costs. Mr. Harris engaged a lawyer, who filed a countersuit for misrepresentation against the water-softener company. It came to nothing. The judgment went against the Harrises.

"At the present moment I have a disconnected water softener, plus a supply of coarse salt and laundry and hand soap, sitting in my basement, for which I owe the finance company $594," Mr. Harris wrote me recently. "Under our present circumstances, it is impossible to pay them. On top of this, I also owe court costs and lawyers' fees. What a mess! It is a problem to which I have no solution."

2

In the mid-thirties, the North American continent was struck by a fad of such compelling force that it is remembered now by social historians as one of the major phenomena of the depression era. This was the dime chain-letter craze, which began in Denver on April 26, 1935. Three days after it started, the post office in that city was forced to add a hundred extra clerks to its staff to handle the landslide of mail. By early May, the continent was in the throes of a chain-letter mania. There were few people, even in the most isolated areas, who did not receive at least one letter. The lunacy reached such proportions that in some towns (Springfield, Missouri, was one) all business was suspended for several days.

The chain-letter principle was old and familiar, but it had hitherto been reserved for good-luck prayers. Now, in the darkest hours of America's travail, when a dime was the monetary symbol of the handout, prayer was replaced by the promise of prosperity. A letter was received containing a list of five names. Within three days the recipient was supposed to make five copies of the letter, deleting the top name and appending his own at the bottom. He mailed these copies to five friends and sent a dime to the name that he struck off. If nobody broke the chain, he would eventually be deluged with a shower of 15,625 dimes—$1,562.50.

Before the fad died away, there were 25-cent letters, dollar letters, and even $10 letters—or, more usually, $10 telegrams. Chain-letter agencies opened up. Actual "factories" came into being to mass-produce the letters. Salesmen peddled chain letters, door to door, and on the phone. For weeks the dime-letter craze was the chief subject of conversation on the continent. Then suddenly, in mid-June, it was over.

Few people had listened to the mathematicians who tried to explain how quickly the saturation point is reached when the chain principle is invoked. Even those whose logic whispered that there must be something wrong could not grasp that it could go wrong so fast. They were certain that they would receive their avalanche of dimes; it was only those who followed after who would be left in the financial cold.

The fact was that, if it took 15,625 persons to contribute $1,562.50 to one person, then a total of 244,140,625 letters would have to be circulated for each of the original 15,625 to receive a like amount. That was more than twice the population of the United States in 1935.

The dime-chain letter, being a form of lottery, was actually illegal in the United States, and steps were taken both there and in Canada to prevent its recurrence. Yet the fad did recur, in the more affluent postwar years, in the form of the pyramid clubs, which made their appearance briefly in the early months of 1949. The pyramid clubs eschewed the mails and charged not a dime but a dollar, which was paid out by new members who attended special pyramid parties.

The clubs worked on the principle of arithmetic progression. The originator (who was usually the only one to make any money) gathered ten friends about him and formed them into a kind of Jacob's ladder, with the tenth man delegated to start the pyramid. This man's job was to persuade six new members to join the club (or two or four—the numbers varied). These six had to get six more—and so on. Each new member paid a dollar to the one ahead of him on the list. The money flowed up through the pyramid until the man at the apex collected the first day's take. On the second day the person on the second level of the pyramid moved up to collect, while, at the bottom, each of the new members was scrounging six more friends. Theoretically the man at the apex could garner more than $2,000 for himself.

Again the public was blind to the realities of mathematical saturation. It was calculated that it would take the entire population of the United States to keep one game going for just twenty days. That explains why the craze rarely lasted more than a week or two in any city it hit. But, during that short period of lunacy, switchboards were jammed with club members seeking new players, traffic often doubled because of the nightly pyramid parties, and theater attendance fell off drastically.

And the pyramid idea did not quite fade away. It was appropriated by the sales agencies as another way of luring new customers. The basic appeal (that somehow you will clean up) and the basic flaws (that the saturation point is swiftly attained) are exactly the same—as the unfortunate Mr. Harris discovered. But the fallacies are still not understood, and a variety of products ranging from coffee and vitamins to vacuum cleaners and even automobiles are being sold today through variations of the technique used to victimize Mr. Harris.

The simplest form of chain-letter selling is the one used by certain wholesale cigarette sales companies. Such companies send out cards promising to mail you 600 cigarettes for only $3.60—an enormous saving. Attached to each card are three tear-off receipts. If you can talk three friends into paying you $3.60 each and signing the receipts, then the company will sell you the cigarettes at the bargain rate. All you have to do is send in the three receipts signed by your friends, together with their money and your own $3.60, and you can take advantage of the offer. On this first sale the company gets $14.40 in advance.

In return, your friends also receive a similar card. If they can each persuade three friends to sign up, then they too will receive 600 cigarettes for the $3.60 they've already paid. The company will get another $10.80.

From the company's point of view, this scheme is foolproof. They never send out 600 cigarettes without getting at least $10.80 in advance—and in some cases more. For the first customers it is an undeniable bargain—as long as they have three friends willing to pay out $3.60. Sooner or later, however, somebody's friendship is going to be seriously bruised when late arrivals discover they have paid $3.60 in advance, but cannot get any cards filled out. These people get nothing for their money.

In sales parlance the chain-letter or pyramid schemes are known as "referral plans" because one customer refers a salesman to another customer. Legitimate leads have always been valued by salesmen and are often paid for; but modern referral plans go a step further when they use the idea as a pure sales device. For instance, Cortez International, which sells a series of kitchen utensils under the name of Wonder

Ware, eases its salesmen through the doorway by the familiar method of pretending that they are advertising men taking a survey. At the close of the sales talk, however, they employ the referral technique, using leading questions to get commitments from their prospects:

"When I came into your home this evening, I told you my job is advertising, and advertising it is. If I told you that this fabulous set of Wonder Ware can be yours for $19.90 through our advertising program, would you give me $19.90 right now?

"About how many Christmas cards did you receive last year? No doubt you sent out as many or even more, right? If I told you that you could own this cookware by simply arranging for me to show this to other people, as I have shown it to you, how many of those friends to whom you sent Christmas cards could you send me to see in the next fifteen months? Thirty?

"How many of those thirty people would give me $19.90 for this cookware, if they had the opportunity? I am certain that you will agree with me that if they were shown what this set could do for them, as I have shown you, they all would give me $19.90, right?

"If I were to give you $10 for each of these thirty people who give me $19.90 for this cookware, you would receive thirty times ten, or $300. Would you have any objections to receiving this money?

"If I were to give you $20 for each of these people, that would be twenty times thirty, or $600. Would you like to receive this money?"

The salesman then returns to his theme and talks about the unusual expense of newspaper and magazine advertising: "Actually, all of the advertisers spend $90 in advertising per year on every person in this country. Since the average family has three people, that is three times ninety, or $270, spent on each family in Canada for advertising. We are willing to spend $270 of advertising money on you. However, in a different way."

He pulls out a small booklet of "advertising certificates."

"For every person you send me to—for each one who gives me $19.90 for this set—you will receive at least $25 of our advertising money. Before I show this program to you, however, I must make two things perfectly clear: First of all, this cookware set stays here this evening. Second, due to the nature of this program, this is the only chance I have of giving you this opportunity."

The prospects are then shown that, for each friend who signs up for the plan, they will earn a $50 rebate. After six have signed up, the cookware will have been paid for. Then the lucky customers will start to make money—$25 for each additional friend who signs up. But to join the scheme, the prospects must sign a conditional sales contract, which commits them to a down payment of $19.90 and fourteen monthly installments of $19.50—a total of almost $300.

In addition, the prospects, as usual, sign a promissory note for the face value of the outstanding balance which is labeled a "negotiable instrument" and can be sold at a discount to any finance company.

An ingenious variation on the referral plan has been used by the Compact Agency of Toronto to sell vacuum cleaners, floor polishers, and carpet sweepers door-to-door. Compact actually promised to pay (and in fact did pay) five dollars in cash to every prospect referred to it by a purchaser—whether the prospect bought anything or not. The following amusing conversation with one of their salesman, relayed to me by a skeptical prospect, gives an idea of how the plan works.

SALESMAN: I want to leave these three appliances with you. All I want you to do is tell your friends about them.

PROSPECT: Come on. Talk English. Tell me what the gimmick is.

SALESMAN: Well, here: you give me $19.80 and I'll give you these three machines. I'll also give you $75.

PROSPECT: *Wh-at?*

SALESMAN: Yes! I'll give $75. Not to you, but this is to help you. This is for promotion.

PROSPECT: How?

SALESMAN: Look—within the next fifteen months all you have to do to have this machine for nothing is to arrange for me to have interviews with fifteen of your friends, exactly like your friends arranged this interview here this morning. To help you make them interested and make them stay home and make them want to listen to me, I provide five dollars for each one of these persons that you name. And for every one who takes a machine, we credit you with $25, so that, if ten or fifteen buy, the machine is paid for.

PROSPECT: What's your security? You've got $19.80 there for the machine and just my promise. . . .

SALESMAN: Oh, no, that's not quite it. Some people aren't honest with us. They're really taking us for a ride. They want to buy the machine for cash and that doesn't interest us. We have to protect our-

selves against such people. If I, for example, had a feeling all you wanted to
do was buy this machine from me, this
morning, I wouldn't sell it to you. Naturally, to protect ourselves we will have
a financing agreement drawn up with a
finance company of our choice for fifteen payments of $17 and change.

PROSPECT: Oh, so you want to sell me your three
machines for two hundred and seventy-
odd dollars and financing?

SALESMAN: That's right.

PROSPECT: What's the price, cash?

SALESMAN: It's $239.

PROSPECT: And you're giving $75 to fifteen people
I'm going to name.

SALESMAN: Right!

PROSPECT: Well, we'll take away another $75 from
$239 and that leaves us with $165. I'll
give you $165 for these three machines.

SALESMAN (*aghast*): Oh no—you can't *do* that!

PROSPECT: I'll give you $20 for the carpet sweeper.
I like it.

SALESMAN: No, no.

PROSPECT: I'll buy the vacuum for $100—whaddya
say?

SALESMAN: No—you can't do that. We're just not
interested. We don't sell for cash. All
we want to do is promote the machine.

PROSPECT: If I have the cash, why should I go
through a finance company and pay
over $270 for something you say is
worth $239?

SALESMAN: It *is* worth $239. That's what you're go-
ing to pay for it two or three years from
now when we get it on the market.

PROSPECT: Maybe. But now I want to buy it for
cash.

SALESMAN: No, no, *no!* It can't be done. You're not
going to get us names.

PROSPECT: Look, if you're selling 1,000 machines
a month like you claim you're doing,
you'll have 12,000 on the market in a
year, and the second year you'll have
120,000.

SALESMAN: That's right. Everybody's buying them.
It's very few people that have to pay
the $17 a month. Usually in three or
four months they've completely finished
paying off the machine and they've
started to make money.

PROSPECT: Okay! If it's working in most cases, then
in about three or four years you're going to have over a million of your vacuum cleaners in Toronto, and I can't
see where you're going to put them.

At this point, the salesman gave up and left—much to the
chagrin of the prospect's wife, who all this time had been
pulling at his coat sleeve, whispering: "Come on! Come on!
Give him the $19.80. It looks terrific!"

There are other variations. One vacuum cleaner company,
Kirby Sommers, guaranteed under its advertising plan: *You
will be paid by check $10 each for two appointments a
month arranged by you with friends who see the Kirby
presentation, regardless of whether a Kirby is placed or not.*

Boris Spremo, an immigrant new to Toronto, thought this

sounded foolproof, so he signed a contract committing himself to $240, which is a good deal to pay for a vacuum cleaner. Alas, he did not pay enough attention to the "Guide for Making Bona Fide Appointments," which left the company many loopholes. Of the eleven appointments he made, he was paid for only two. A variety of excuses, all valid, was used by the company for refusing payment on the other nine: the wife left the room during the demonstration; the prospect was a bachelor; the prospect had no phone; the salesman was late for the appointment and so it was not kept; the prospect lived under the same roof as another prospect; the prospect already had a vacuum cleaner.

The chain-letter method of selling has been refined and revised over the years, so that very little is left to chance. Few companies, for instance, take a gamble on customers composing their own letters to entice friends. The companies write the letter. For people who are too lazy to copy a letter, they supply what appears to be a typewritten letter. The one used recently by Water Conditioners of Canada went like this:

Dear ———:

Could you use some extra money? We are participating in a new profit-sharing plan that we liked so well we took the liberty of recommending you to the people who originated it.

They have provided us with the means of making money without any cash outlay; nor do we have to sell anything.

What impressed us most was the absence of any "gimmicks" or "high pressure." Although it is extremely simple, it would be impossible to explain it by telephone or letter, so if they should telephone you for an appointment, be sure and look into it. You won't regret it.

The same company supplied a series of postscripts to be written in by hand to give these letters a more personal touch. Here are some samples:

"Don't miss hearing this, it's really good."

"Hear this out, and let me know how you like it."

"We think this is a good opportunity."

"Be sure to look into it."

"It pays to listen."

But this still wasn't enough. The company also supplied each customer with a card of instructions entitled *What to Say If Your Friends Call.*

If your friends call, tell them, "This is a Money-Making Program—and my friends in this program are making a lot of Extra Money!"

Some of your friends may be a little inquisitive, Tell Them the Truth.

Say, "I don't want to make a mystery out of this—but I don't want to confuse you either. It'll be to Your Benefit for a qualified person to explain this to you, and then, You Won't Feel Under Obligation to anyone.

"All I can tell you is this—It's an Honest to Goodness Opportunity for You to Make Some Extra Money.

"We Like It—and if I didn't know You'd Enjoy this—and it was Worth Your Time to Listen too—I wouldn't recommend this to You."

This will stop your friends from asking any more questions —Remember, the Less you Say—the Better!

Always talk Enthusiastically about the Money-Making Program—and DO NOT TALK ABOUT THE WATER SOFTENER! BE ENTHUSIASTIC! — IT'S CONTAGIOUS.

Thus do thousands of people unwittingly find themselves playing the traditional role of Steer man in a game that is more widespread than the Duke or the Payoff.

3

A more direct form of the referral plan is the you-be-a-salesman scheme that removes the middleman entirely and threatens to turn half the populace into hucksters peddling electric organs, fire-alarm systems, and food supplements to one another.

In December 1960, this advertisement appeared in the Toronto *Telegram* under "Construction Workers":

STEADY year-round employment with Safety Equipment Company. Salary and bonus. Must be over 21, married and own a car and prepare to start work immediately. For personal interview, telephone ————.

This ad was placed by Vanguard Systems of Canada Ltd., a company that sells fire alarms; but those who applied did not learn this until much later. First, they found themselves closeted in a small room with several other men for their "personal interview."

A long, ambiguous sales lecture followed. There was talk about a sales-training course. There were flattering references to an enormous parent corporation that worked with jet aircraft. There was the usual mumbo jumbo about surveys, tests, public service, and, finally, the need for fire protection. There was a fifteen-minute tape-recorded sales talk. There were display cards, brochures, photographs. Finally, the men were allowed to see what they were supposed to sell —a set of six chromium-plated bells that worked on the thermostatic principle. They were told they would sell these bells to the public for $229.95 a set—an incredibly high price.

Then came the denouement: to qualify, these lucky "salesmen" would themselves have to own a set of these alarms. The price, it was indicated, was a mere $14.95. The contracts revealed, however, that each man would pay $14.95 in cash and sign up to pay the remaining $215 in eighteen monthly installments. However, they were assured, they would not have to pay the rest because they could easily get nine of their friends to buy alarm bells too. They would get $25 credit for each sale, and after the ninth sale the money would start to roll in. And they could use the same sales gimmick on their friends! Their friends could become salesmen too, and sell their friends! The possibilities were endless.

A similar advertisement placed about the same time in the "Help Wanted, Female" column, was slightly more direct in its message:

WOMEN   part-time, to do telephone soliciting at home for console chord organs; 1–2 hours a day and you can own one and earn extra money, commission basis.

The women who answered this ad discovered they must each buy a "demonstrator" organ for $149 before the company would give them the job. Having done this, they would be paid $10 commission for every organ they sold; but until they bought an organ they could not go to work.

These operations are small-time, however, when compared with the wave of food-supplement schemes which began to sweep the continent as early as 1958 and 1959 and which were built up on the pyramid concept. There have been several, but the best known, perhaps, has been that of Nutri-Bio.

Like the other food-supplement schemes, Nutri-Bio managed to combine two of the wackiest traditions in the social history of North America: the universal get-rich-quick scheme and the universal get-healthy food fad. In its latter aspects, this has certainly rivaled Dr. McCoy's orange-juice mania, *circa* 1925, and Gayelord Hauser's molasses-and-yoghurt craze, *circa* 1949.

When Nutri-Bio moved into Toronto in 1960, after sweeping the United States and the Canadian west coast, it was said to have reached total annual sales of $100 million. Within twelve months there were few people who were not aware of it: those who weren't actually selling Nutri-Bio were on the receiving end of phone calls from people who were trying to sell it.

Nutri-Bio is supposed to contain almost every known vitamin, in addition to other nutritional aids. The idea of an all-in-one pill that compounds minerals and trace elements, as well as vitamins, has been received by nutritionists with as little enthusiasm as has the general thesis, promulgated by the food-supplement hucksters, that the populace is generally underfed and undernourished and will continue to be so unless it spoon-feeds itself with daily doses of the universal panacea.

Food faddism, however, has its own evangelism; and when this is attended by the evangelism that seems to accompany most modern-day salesmanship, the results can be awesome. In Nutri-Bio's ingenious scheme of things, every customer was automatically a salesman, and, since every customer believed (or supposedly believed) in the bodily advantages of the product—believed it, indeed, with a fierceness that resisted all cynicism—the effect was augmented. Nutri-Bio sales meetings, which were held all over town, had a religious fervor to them. The light of pure faith shone from the eyes of the sales apostles as they preached the twin gospels of Perfect Health and Unlimited Wealth.

In addition, the company marshaled an enviable troika of Hollywood stars to trumpet the merits of its product. Mr. Robert Cummings, toothpaste smile firmly in place, was high on the Pantheon as a vice-president. His role was quite plainly that of Mr. Eternal Youth. Mr. Harry Von Zell was rung in, via film clips, as the Average Bumbler, who takes Nutri-Bio "just in case." Mr. Marvin Miller, of *The Millionaire*, enacted his TV role on a sound track played at the revival meetings. "If I've ever heard of a million-dollar proposition, this is it," said Mr. Miller's recorded voice. A glance at the expensive Nutri-Bio literature suggested that, of the two concepts Nutri-Bio was promoting, Wealth was proving to be somewhat stronger than Health.

The men at the top of the complicated Nutri-Bio structure did not appear to be taking any undue risks. Their technique was to corner customers by advertising for salesmen. Since every salesman was pledged to buy a year's supply of Nutri-Bio, "in order to believe in the product," and since every salesman had to pay, initially, the full retail price of $26 before he could start making money, it is difficult to see how the insiders could lose.

More than sixty per cent of the retail price of this food supplement went into sales costs. In addition, the salesmen had to pay for their promotion kits as well as for other sales literature. One wondered, sometimes, whether Nutri-Bio wasn't also in the publishing business. A slender twenty-one-page pamphlet entitled *Your Financial Opportunities*, which explained the sales setup, was sold to the disciples at fifty cents a copy. Many a paperback novel sells for less.

The scheme itself, when reduced to its bare essentials, was fairly simple. The more Nutri-Bio one ordered in a batch, the less one paid for it—hence the profit margin increased for those who bought in large quantities. A man who bought a mere $276 worth a month, for instance, received a forty per cent discount. In Nutri-Bio's quasi-military establishment, he was called a corporal. But those who climbed to the dizzy heights of generalship were awarded a sixty per cent discount. These people had to invest $13,000 a month in Nutri-Bio. Some of them had basements full of it.

The logic of the sales story, as enthusiastically explained at the revival meetings, was somewhat more shaky. Housewives were told, for instance, that if they made three calls on their friends each week they could earn $110 a month—and for only three hours' work. Three calls a day could bring in $828 a month. This presupposed that every call would produce a sale; that each call would take only one hour; and that the list of one's accommodating friends was unlimited. The evangelists airily dismissed this problem, however, and blandly went on to show that, when the repeat orders started pouring in, a housewife who worked three hours a week could make $2,200 a month.

But this was small potatoes in the Nutri-Bio Vision of Health and Wealth. It was much more lucrative to become an armchair wholesaler or "sponsor" by persuading one's friends to go out to sell Nutri-Bio, too. These friends would buy from you in job lots, thus allowing you to order larger and larger quantities of Nutri-Bio. When one of these friends hit the $13,000 mark and in his turn became a general, then he could order directly from the factory—but you would still receive a two per cent commission on every sale he made. The implication was that the time would come when you could just sit at home and let the money roll in.

Once again the laws of mathematics suggested that before

long everybody in the land would be selling Nutri-Bio to everybody else. This is, in effect, what began to happen. By the spring of 1961, classified ads were appearing in the Toronto papers offering consignments of Nutri-Bio to any taker at half price. The saturation point had been reached. By 1962 the company was in financial difficulties in Canada. The pyramid idea, however, had by no means run its course. Even as the basements began to be glutted with Nutri-Bio, a new set of get-rich-quick letters started to circulate in the mails. A friend of mine received one from Vancouver.

"Look at this letter from George and Joan," he said, pulling a crumpled billet-doux from his pocket. "It's in George's handwriting, but it doesn't sound like either of them. . . ."

Dear Tim and Mary:

This is just a short note to let you know of "something to your advantage." I can't tell you much in a letter about this—the name I will give you to contact will give you the details. We were very fortunate in finding out and going into this ourselves.

There is an opportunity of making over $1,000 a month. . . . There is no actual selling involved. . . . Sorry to be so mysterious. . . . You have nothing to lose. . . .

The phrases had a familiar ring to them, for they were remarkably similar to the ones the Reverend Mr. Harris had been given to use on his friends. The firm in this case turned out to be Nutri-Foods of Canada Ltd., and it was apparently following in the footsteps of its various predecessors. As long as friendship is considered a salable commodity, like vitamins, letters like this will continue to clog the mails as they did during the dime-letter craze of 1935.

6

How to Lose Big Money in Your Spare Time

On a sunny morning in mid-April 1959, a crowd of more than a hundred women choked McGill College Avenue in Montreal and tried to enter the offices of two companies, Yarncraft Industries Ltd. and Fair Isle Knitting Ltd. They did not get in because both companies had gone out of business. The women departed disconsolate and angry. Behind them they left, piled high against the windows, a small mountain of shopping bags and paper cartons containing bundles of knitted wear for which they had no further use.

In Montreal alone there were some hundreds of these women—working-class housewives who had been sold $28 knitting machines at approximately $400 and told they could make big money in their spare time. In Toronto there were more of them, perhaps thousands, and throughout eastern Canada, in small towns and villages, there were others. For months after the two companies folded their tents, the newspapers carried reports of lawsuits brought by finance companies against men and women who had bought these machines and could not or would pay the installments on them. The finance companies almost invariably won, and to this day there are people, some with their wages garnisheed, paying installments on useless machines, which they once hoped would make their fortune.

The case of Martin and Helga Bagchus, an immigrant couple in Toronto, is fairly typical. They received a card in their mailbox one day addressed *To the Homemaker* with the words: "Ladies! Don't Miss This Wonderful Opportunity! See Inside!"

The message inside was signed by Susan Adams of Yarncraft Industries, and it read:

EARN MONEY IN YOUR SPARE TIME AT HOME!
Knit for us in your spare hours at home and make $50 to $150 extra money every month!

Complete training provided to those who qualify. It's pleasant and satisfying. If you have 15 or more hours to spare per week, send the postage paid card below for full details (no obligation).

Like thousands of others who were pressed for cash, Mrs. Bagchus mailed in the card. Presently a Mr. Bayda turned up at her door and explained that his company would sell wool to her at the wholesale rate of thirty-five cents an ounce and buy it back from her at sixty cents an ounce. She was to make baby garments. Of course, to make them properly, she would have to buy a knitting machine; but the proceeds of the knitting would more than pay for the machine—or so Mr. Bayda said.

Mr. Bayda had three documents for Mrs. Bagchus to sign. The first was an "Application for Home Knitting Contract" from Yarncraft Industries. Under this contract, which was approved by Bayda as "Personnel Representative," Yarncraft agreed to supply Mrs. Bagchus with enough orders for woolen goods to fill her spare hours at home. She was to follow the patterns the company sent her, deliver each order in one complete shipment within thirty days, and make a profit, for knitting these orders, of four dollars per pound of knitted goods. She would have the privilege of purchasing fine-quality yarns at a substantial discount, and she was to receive instruction in the art of knitting.

There was an additional statement, to which Mrs. Bagchus paid scant attention: "I further understand and agree that if I am granted a Home Knitting Contract, this contract will become a separate business entity."

The second document was a purchase order from the Trans World Machine Company. This was nothing more than a name used by Fair Isle Knitting, which operated from the same address as Yarncraft. Trans World agreed to sell Mrs. Bagchus a knitting machine for $399, of which $39 was the down payment; the balance was to be repaid at the rate of $22.50 a month for sixteen months, presumably from the profits of her knitting, though nowhere on the purchase order was this mentioned. The machine was unconditionally guaranteed for two years and there was a twenty-year guarantee that needles and other parts would be available.

There were two other significant paragraphs.

I further agree to sign a Conditional Sales Contract and a promissory note for the protection of Trans World Machine Co. or its agents or assignees. I also agree to make the payments as set out in the Conditional Sales Contract, irrespective of whether the knitting machine hereby purchased is used for personal use or for the earning of income.

All verbal or written agreements not mentioned on the face of this contract are void and no agent has authority to change, alter or add to this contract in any particular.

The third document was a conditional sales contract, to which was attached a promissory note for the amount of the outstanding balance—$360. Both Mr. and Mrs. Bagchus were asked to sign this document. This note was immediately endorsed to the Model Finance Corporation by the Trans World Machine Co.

Many of the women who had bought these machines had great trouble with them and with Yarncraft Industries. In spite of what they had been told, it was difficult to make much money sewing baby garments at home. Many garments were rejected. The yarn was full of knots. The machines did not always work well. The patterns seemed to get harder and harder.

Mrs. Bagchus struggled through one order. Her husband took it down to the office of Yarncraft and asked for his money. A girl at the office said that the man who issued the checks was not in. She promised that the company would mail it. Mr. Bagchus persisted. It seemed strange, he said, that such a large company as this one should have only one man to issue checks. He received his money, but others who were also waiting did not.

One month later, when Mrs. Bagchus had completed her second order, the following letter arrived in the mail.

Dear Knitter:
Due to adjustments and problems as a result of reorgani-

zation, we find it necessary to close the Wool Buy Back Operation until April 13th, 1959. At this time we will begin to service you and bring your account up to date.

But there was no reopening. A few days later a second letter was sent out by Yarncraft explaining that "it is with the greatest regret that we now find it necessary to advise you that we are suspending operations. The demand for our knitted goods has fallen off drastically. As a result, we have found it necessary to dispose of merchandise unprofitably. We have made every effort to continue but now find ourselves completely out of funds. . . ."

Fair Isle Knitting Ltd. and the Trans World Machine Company also suspended business. The entire sales operation had lasted less than two years. But in this short period several hundred salesmen had sold several thousand Japanese-made knitting machines with a wholesale value of about $28 for $400 apiece.

The Bagchuses had made one payment on their machine, but they had made no more. Very quickly they began to receive letters from the Model Finance Corporation demanding payment of their delinquent account. When the Bagchuses refused to pay, the letters grew tougher. Within two months the finance company was threatening legal action. That fall the Bagchuses found themselves facing a lawsuit in Division Court. They hired a lawyer to fight the case.

In court the following facts were brought out:

First, the Bagchuses had signed a promissory note, and this promissory note, detached from the contract for the knitting machine, was presented as a separate document. The finance company said it knew nothing of a knitting contract. All it knew was that it had bought a negotiable paper from Trans World Machine Company.

Second, the contract with Yarncraft Industries was shown

to be a "separate business entity." Mrs. Bagchus had signed a document acknowledging that fact. It had, on paper, nothing to do with the sale of a knitting machine. Yarncraft was a separate company; it did not sell knitting machines.

Third, Mrs. Bagchus had also signed a document agreeing to make the payments for the knitting machine, whether it was used "for personal use or for the earning of an income," and she had further agreed that any verbal or written agreement not on the contract was meaningless.

From the legal point of view, then, the case was clear. The Bagchuses had bought something and promised to pay for it. They had signed a legal document to this effect. The judgment was in favor of the finance company.

"I am sorry for your people," the judge told the Bagchuses' lawyer, "but my conclusion is that I cannot do anything for them. I think this man and woman allowed themselves to be talked into a contract without any investigation whatever as to the reliability of the parties with whom they were doing business and without investigating the market value of the machine they were buying. This involves only the contract and the promissory note. The commercial world would soon fall apart if promissory notes were tossed about. . . ."

The Bagchuses appealed the case and lost again, as did a good many others in Ontario and Quebec who found themselves being dunned by finance companies for payments on knitting machines that were worthless to them. No legal action, of course, was taken against the men who formed Fair Isle Knitting Ltd. One of them turned up again in Toronto a few years later, running an interesting organization called the Home-Service Club, designed, he said, to protect the public from racketeers who preyed upon unsuspecting housewives. "There are door-to-door racketeers just moving from one part of the city to another," he told the press piously. He gained a small platoon of new customers that way.

The knitting story, of course, is not unique. All across North America, advertisements are being placed in the classified columns and mailing pieces are being stuffed under doors to tell housewives that they can make big money in their spare time. The Better Business Bureau warns consistently against this "home work," as it is called, but the lure of spare cash is hard to resist.

Fair Isle Knitting Ltd. had scarcely suspended operations when this advertisement appeared in Eastern Canadian papers.

WANTED: Ladies to do easy sewing at home. Make up to $26 per week. Write Box 491. Adelaide P.O. Toronto

---

The women who answered this ad—and they were in the thousands—were told that their applications had been carefully considered and that a company known as Bunny's Baby Shoes would like to employ them to sew baby shoes. It was easy work, and the company would send along a "test kit" for two dollars.

This money was only a deposit: "If you decide to sew Bunny's shoes, we will refund the $2 in full, after you have completed your first 24 pairs."

For her two dollars, each woman got a few pieces of felt. Since finished shoes of similar style were retailing for around one dollar, this was no bargain. And the three plans that the company offered for selling the shoes were such that few sensible women would accept them.

There were two plans under which the women were asked to find retail outlets for the shoes—or else sell them to their friends. At the prices quoted, it was difficult to understand how a profit could be made. In the third plan the company itself offered to buy the finished shoes, "if in our opinion they are properly sewn to our instructions." I asked an expert seamstress to try to sew a pair of these sample shoes, and she reported it was almost impossible to do so according to instructions.

But the company was certainly making a healthy profit selling the two-dollar test kits, through the lure of easy profits for spare-time work.

2

In the winter of 1959–60, small-town and ethnic newspapers all over Ontario received an order for six consecutive insertions under the classified section of business opportunities; the order came from a company called General Merchandising Distributors of Canada, a "Division of General Nylon Corporation Limited," a Toronto firm. The advertisement, which brought hundreds of replies, and which was also to bring heartache, despair, and financial ruin to scores of people, read:

> PART-TIME STEADY   delivery work in this area. No selling required. Canadian corporation distributing nationally advertised products requires a local resident to make light deliveries to established accounts in this area. No experience necessary. Applicant must have good driving record, be reliable, sober and honest, have transportation in the form of a car or light truck and have $1,200 cash available. Could be handled by someone presently employed.

Among those who answered one of these ads was a couple I shall refer to as Garry and Madeleine Hill. In due course, they received a call from a Mr. Rose who said he was from the contract division of the personnel department of General Merchandising. Mr. Rose had a voice that sounded like a mortician's—quiet and reserved. He said he would like to

visit the Hills' home since this was a job for a responsible
man and it was necessary to see the home surroundings. He
explained that there was a sizable amount of money involved
and the company had to be careful about the people it chose
to represent its interests. He made an appointment for one
p.m. the following day.

The interview with Mr. Rose took several hours. He explained that his organization placed racks of nationally advertised products—ranging from Blue Jay Foot Pads to Vicks
Vaporub—in drugstores and other outlets. They were seeking trusted employees who would service these racks regularly—keeping them stocked with merchandise, checking
the sales, and sending the cash to the company.

Mr. Rose spoke quietly, in the manner of a man interviewing applicants for an executive post. He had, he said, investigated twelve people in the past twenty-four hours and
recommended only four; but he implied that the Hills stood
a good chance. He was not interested in salesmen, he explained emphatically. If that was the sort of thing they were
looking for, he said, they could look elsewhere; the company
simply wanted people it could trust to service its accounts.
His opening remarks were in a disarmingly low key.

"Your income may not be very high at first," Mr. Rose explained. "For instance, say a druggist buys $30 worth of
merchandise a week. Now, your percentage would be just
twenty-five per cent of that. We would start you off servicing
just ten stores. I don't want to paint an unrealistic picture,
you understand, so I'm keeping the estimates low. But of
course if any druggist didn't do $30 worth of business a
week, well, he just wouldn't be in business very long, would
he?"

The Hills nodded. They had reckoned mentally that they
would make a minimum of $75 a week if these figures were
correct.

Mr. Rose then began to question Garry Hill closely. Was he a good driver? Had he had any accidents? Could he supply references? Had he ever collected money before? Did he feel he could handle this kind of work? Mr. Hill nodded eagerly.

"It's a position of trust," Mr. Rose explained. His company absolutely had to have honest responsible people doing this collecting. The Hills understood that, didn't they?

Mr. Rose then got down to brass tacks. He explained that Garry Hill would visit each drugstore on his route once a week and replace from his stock the items missing in the display rack. The druggist would have a sheet with all the items listed, and every time he sold one, he would check it off. This would show Garry how much money the druggist owed. The money would be paid to Garry in his name and he would deposit it in his own bank account. Then he would send a check to the company, minus his twenty-five per cent commission. In this way the company would know how many items to ship out the following week.

It did not take Mr. and Mrs. Hill long to realize that under this system there were a dozen ways in which the company could be cheated. No wonder they were looking for honest responsible people! Anybody with a grain of larceny in his makeup could juggle the figures to his own advantage.

Mr. Rose then explained that the company would require a kind of bond from the Hills—provided he was able to recommend them for the job. He did not use the word "bond"; he explained that it was a kind of insurance, since the dealer would be handling so much money. It was a sign of good faith, and also, of course, it was needed to cover the cost of the goods that the company would be shipping by express. Mr. Hill must remain with the company for one year, making an initial deposit of $1,200 in cash. After the year was up, this $1,200 would be returned to him.

He brought out an application form for Garry Hill to fill out: the form was a stiff one. It asked for innumerable references and background details. It asked: *Do you think you can work under your own supervision? Do you think you will like route work? If so, would you consider it full-time at a later date?* Obviously, General Merchandising was looking for solid citizens.

When the application was completed, Mr. Rose said that it was one of the best he had seen.

"I usually hesitate to recommend anyone," he explained, "but I'll try to rush this through for you. There's a board meeting this afternoon."

He produced a contract for Garry Hill to sign. The contract called for the "dealer" to give the company $1,200, for which the company, on its part, would supply display trays in ten stores. The addresses or locations of these stores was not specified, and Mr. Rose seemed to be a little vague about where they would be.

Indeed, the whole contract seemed to be vague except for the mention of the $1,200. There wasn't even a place for a witness to the signatures.

Mr. Rose asked if it would be convenient to give him the $1,200 then and now.

"You mean you want our money before our application is accepted?" asked Garry Hill.

"Oh, well," said Mr. Rose, "if your application is refused, your money will be refunded."

Mr. Hill explained that his money was tied up in bonds and that it would take him a few days to get the cash. Could Mr. Rose leave a copy of the contract? No, Mr. Rose could not leave anything. He made another appointment and left.

The Hills, of course, had no intention of paying Mr. Rose a cent. They were not even married to each other and their names were not Hill. I had engaged them to give me a full report on these strange ads that had been appearing in the newspapers.

But dozens and perhaps hundreds of others did give Mr. Rose and his associates $1,200. In every instance the results were the same. Little if any merchandise was shipped to them. Either there were no drugstores at all or, if there were, they were in remote areas so far away that it was almost impossible to service them. More than that, these stores did not wish to be serviced. They didn't want the racks in the first place.

This "rack merchandise" deal is an old and trusted racket. The principals in General Merchandising, several of whom eventually went to jail for fraud, had been involved for years in a variety of similar schemes. The basic principle was always the same. The victims thought they were going to make easy money servicing racks of merchandise, or vending machines, in their spare time. To get the job they had to put up some cash of their own. They did not see this cash again, and the company swiftly moved or went out of business. If the victims did receive merchandise, it did not begin to cover the cost of their initial investment. If racks or vending machines were actually placed in stores, they were almost always in impossible, nonpaying locations. Those who lost a mere $1,200 on this particular scheme were fortunate. The stakes are often much higher.

3

So powerful is the pull of the distributor-franchise racket, so powerful the urge to make easy money in one's spare time, that in any month and in any newspaper you can usually find advertisements for "once-in-a-lifetime opportunities" promising an immediate cash return on the applicant's investment—"absolutely no selling or canvassing". . . "distributorship granted only after personal interview". . . "opportunity for right man to service established retail outlets.". . .

Not all of this advertising is larcenous, but there is much, like that of General Merchandising, which invites larceny on the part of the applicant.

Indeed, it is well to move cautiously when investigating "real business opportunities," as three recent authentic cases, all in my own neighborhood, demonstrate.

In the spring of 1961, for instance, a retired Englishman named Clifford Smith answered such an ad. A few days later, a man named Anthony Aquanno dropped around to explain the deal to him. If Mr. Smith had read the newspapers carefully, he might have known that this same Aquanno was out on bail, pending fraud charges against him and his colleagues, for the General Merchandising franchise racket recorded above. But who remembers names? Aquanno was shortly to go to jail, but Smith and his wife had no inkling of that.

All they knew was that he was demonstrating a new patent medicine called Cup'N Seltzer, which he said would be a fast seller in the drugstores. A week later Aquanno brought his boss, Wolf Yess, and before Yess left he had almost $1,500 of the Smiths' money.

The Smiths might have been less ready to give Yess any money had they known the number of franchise companies —most of them now defunct—with which he had been associated in the past. The Better Business Bureau had in its files at least six, dealing in franchise merchandise ranging from gum machines to heated potato chips.

Yess explained that the present deal would be very lucrative for Mr. Smith. He would start him off with fifty stores. All Mr. Smith would have to do would be to place racks of Cup'N Seltzer in these stores and then collect a weekly profit from the proprietors. As is so often the case, he was vague about the locations, but he was a fast talker. Mr. Smith signed a contract and paid Yess $1,470.

It is intriguing to see what Smith got for his money. He got a few pieces of paper explaining the deal. He got a list of fifty supposedly bona fide "choice" locations in which to set up his racks of merchandise. He got fifty units of Cup'N Seltzer, each unit containing forty-two 10-cent tablets. And he got a rubber stamp. In short, he got merchandise worth little more than $210 *retail*.

Of the fifty stores he was given, seventeen wanted no part of the deal from the outset. The others took the merchandise, but it failed to move. The stores began to throw them out. Yet, even if Mr. Smith had sold them all, he would have lost money. This did not come home to him, however, before Yess had sold him more merchandise at various prices. Finally, the scales dropped from Mr. Smith's eyes and he began to ask for his money back. He is still trying, vainly, to get it.

Another man who answered an advertisement for Business Opportunities was John Murray, of Scarborough, a Toronto suburb. The ad asked for a $5,000 investment, and Mr. Murray thought he had nothing to lose by answering it. He was wrong. It was to cost him $1,800, plus legal fees.

This ad was placed by Infra Pac Systems, and the man who came to his door, a Mr. Wilkinson, explained it glibly and convincingly. Mr. Murray would be given a list of six hotel bars to service with toasted sandwiches. In each bar he would place a small Infra Pac oven. He would supply the sandwiches, which the oven would toast. The company would supply the little ovens and packages for the sandwiches. All Mr. Murray needed to do was to service the bars and collect the profits, which would keep rolling in.

Mr. Murray signed a contract for a "distributorship" and laid $1,800 on the line for six little ovens, five thousand sandwich bags, five hundred table menus, and fifty display menus. That was not the full price. He promised to pay a total of $4,500 for merchandise not worth a fraction of the cost.

But Mr. Murray was not given the list of hotels which had ostensibly signed contracts with Infra Pac. Nor was he given any merchandise.

After two weeks of silence, he became worried. He tried to reach the company's president, Charles Turner. Mr. Turner was difficult to find since the company kept moving its location. When Mr. Murray finally reached him by phone, he told Turner he wanted his money back. Turner asked him to wait a few days and "everything would be fine." Mr. Murray waited and waited but heard nothing. When his patience became exhausted, he hired a lawyer and sued. It took two years and five months for the case to come to trial. Mr. Murray won in a breeze. The judge awarded him a total of $2,687.25, the additional award being for costs and loss of wages.

But did John Murray get his money? He did not. Charles Turner has vanished. Even if he is found, it is doubtful if he will have the $2,687.25. Mr. Murray was left holding the sandwich bags.

A somewhat different scheme was offered to Mr. Robert Kastelik, in January, 1962, by an organization called International Fibercraft Systems, Ltd. Mr. Kastelik also answered an ad which promised him an income, and was interviewed presently by a Sam Miller, who told him, he says, that he would soon be a millionaire. All Mr. Kastelik had to do was install, in service stations and other outlets, spraying equipment which would beautify old upholstery and automobile interiors through a fabric spray called Fabricote. Fibercraft offered to supply all the equipment, and three excellent locations, for $500. Mr. Kastelik was to receive seventy-five per cent of all fees collected.

He signed a contract promising to pay $500, and an additional $128.90 in interest. Here is what he got for his money: one forty-pound pressure compressor with a one-horsepower motor; one spray gun; one glass jar; twenty-five pounds of assorted fibers; one gallon of adhesive; one roll of masking tape; two brushes; a receipt book and five hundred mimeographed pamphlets about Fibercraft. For $500 this is no bargain.

Mr. Kastelik discovered it was even less of a bargain when two of the dealers with whose names he'd been supplied backed out and a third produced no business. Kastelik tried other garages, but all of them told him the same thing: the prices Fibercraft wanted him to charge (and he had signed a contract agreeing to respect these prices) were too high.

Meanwhile the company had sold his contract to Federated Discount, which had no connection with it but which was certainly interested in collecting the money. There is nothing illegal in this. The men who run Fibercraft are still walking the streets; they did what they promised—no more. They did not make Mr. Kastelik a millionaire, but, then, they did not guarantee on paper that they would. So much for another real business opportunity.

7

The Frustrations of Operative 67

I have in my employ a comely young housewife known to the readers of my newspaper and magazine columns as Operative 67. (To reveal her true identity would be to dilute her effectiveness.) Operative 67, to be blunt, is a spy and a good one. She has the ability to look either glamorous or dowdy as the occasion demands and, though she has a keen and skeptical mind, she can appear to be as gullible or as dense as necessity or sales technique requires. Much of her work for me, however, consists of frustrations—of trying to accomplish feats above and beyond the call of duty, such as trying to get sued by a vitamin company or trying to buy a vacuum cleaner advertised at $12.95 or trying to find out how to make big money as a Family Counsellor. Five of her adventures in frustration are chronicled here.

One of the Operative's more hilarious adventures occurred when I asked her to find out what an encyclopaedia costs. "But it's simple," she said. "I'll just write a letter to an encyclopaedia company and ask for a price list." And she typed out the following letter to the Encyclopaedia Americana.

Dear Sir:

I am interested in buying a set of your encyclopaedia. I do not want a salesman to call on me. As I intend to pay cash, would you please forward your price list for the set of books.

To her surprise and amusement, the Encyclopaedia Americana did not send her a price list by return mail. Instead, the Operative received a phone call from a Mr. Scott, who explained carefully that he was not a salesman. "I just work in the office," Mr. Scott announced.

"We're just getting the program under way," began Mr. Scott, enthusiastically, and then he started to deliver the standard Encyclopaedia Americana sales pitch, which actually got under way many, many years ago.

"What's the price?" the Operative asked, breaking in.

Scott said he would have to talk that over with the office. Could they not send a man around to "explain the program"?

The Operative said she didn't want any explanation—just the price.

Mr. Scott parried the question. Actually, he said, there were several prices and, of course, "a great deal of equipment."

The Operative explained that the letter meant what it said. She did not wish any "equipment" (she had an impression of barbells and hand grips at this point). She just wanted an encyclopaedia. She said she could not understand why he wouldn't know the price.

Mr. Scott was cornered. "It would be in the neighborhood of $400," he admitted, finally.

"*This is a price?*" the Operative asked. "What do you mean, 'neighborhood'? Is that your cheapest set or your most expensive or what? Can't you give me a firm price?"

Mr. Scott described it as the "second set." The first set, he said, was "around $600."

"Is the $400 set your cheapest?" the Operative asked.

Mr. Scott, bobbing and weaving nicely, countered with the remark that "other merchandise" was involved.

The Operative asked him if there were more than two sets, and Mr. Scott admitted that there were only two. He said, again, he would like to send someone around to explain.

The Operative told him not to bother. Then she asked again: "Is $400 your cheapest price?"

"Yes," countered Mr. Scott, "with the other merchandise." *What* other merchandise, the Operative wanted to know.

Mr. Scott said there were other books. The Operative asked him to be specific. Mr. Scott mentioned a dictionary and a Bible. He added that his firm might want to use her name in advertising and he implied that this would result in a bargain rate for the Operative. Again, he pleaded to be allowed to send a man around to explain what kind of an arrangement they could make.

"Look," said the Operative, "I'm not interested in all that. I just want to know the price of the set. There's no use in sending a salesman around."

Mr. Scott insisted he was not a salesman. In fact, he said, there was no sales staff: he merely wanted someone to drop around and explain the special promotional scheme his firm had just launched.

"Just get me a price and cut out all the gabble," said the Operative impatiently.

But Mr. Scott could not do that. He said he would have

to "discuss it" and call back. It was two hours before he did so. Then, finally, he had a price. Operative 67 could buy a set of the encyclopaedia for $249.50.

But when a second operative phoned some time later and asked the price of a set of the Encyclopaedia Americana she was told, after some discussion, that it was $10 a volume or $300 for a set of thirty.

Meanwhile, Operative 67 had written four other encyclopaedia companies identical letters. None sent her a complete price list; in fact, only one answered in writing and that was P. F. Collier and Son Limited, who told her simply and directly that the price, cash, was $245.50.

Again I asked a second operative to check this by phone and again she was given a different story. She was told there was a "special price" of $369.50 on Collier's Encyclopaedia. (Salesmen at the doorstep were quoting that week a "regular price" of $450.) The special price included a set of the Junior Classics and a Bible. My Operative could not find out what the cost was without these extras. She was told that there was nobody in the office who could tell her and, though she tried for several days, she was not able to get the information.

Representatives of two other companies, the Encyclopaedia Britannica and the American People's Encyclopaedia, phoned the Operative. They were not salesmen, they insisted. One described himself as a "manager"; another as simply a "representative." The Operative was able, finally, to get some prices from them, but there did not appear to be a price list as there is for most books. The Britannica sent her a brochure, but this did not list prices either. When my secretary called, she met with similar frustrations. The Britannica flatly refused to give her a price over the telephone.

The World Book Encyclopaedia did not phone. Instead, a Mrs. Brigham knocked on the Operative's door, brief case in hand. She said she just happened to be passing by the Operative's apartment. She explained that Mr. Haven, the district supervisor, had given her the Operative's letter—he thought perhaps she didn't want a high-pressure salesman, but he was sure the Operative wouldn't mind Mrs. Brigham.

The Operative would not let Mrs. Brigham in, but she found she could do nothing to prevent her rattling through the World Book sales pitch. "But what's the price?" the Operative would ask from time to time, and Mrs. Brigham would counter that she had a few things to demonstrate first. It is pointless to report the entire discussion, which went on and on and on, but the Operative did finally get a rock bottom price for the World Book: $154 cash, without extras. It was, she reports, an exhausting inquiry.

2

Another tough assignment that I handed the Operative resulted in three full weeks of frustration.

"Operative 67," I said to her, "here is an advertisement of President Electric Ltd., 420 Dupont Street. It seems they are emptying their warehouse to make room for new merchandise. To do this they are offering tremendous savings on their present stock of brand-name appliances.

"Here, for instance, is a 'famous name brand vacuum cleaner,' which they are offering at the ridiculously low price of $12.95 each.

"Now, Operative 67, here is your assignment: *try to buy one of these vacuum cleaners.*"

It seemed a simple task, but twenty-one days later the Operative returned, empty-handed.

"I've done everything possible," she told me. "I've even

signed a conditional sales contract. But I can't get the vacuum cleaner. They just don't seem to want to sell it to me."

Her story was a lengthy one, but I shall try to condense it here to essentials.

A few days after the Operative answered the ad, a Mr. P. Leufer of President Electric arrived at her door, carrying the $12.95 machine with him in a cardboard box. He gave a brief demonstration.

"Fine!" said the Operative. "I'll take it!" and she handed him $15.

Mr. Leufer said that he was awfully sorry, but he had no change. He said, however, that he would have the machine shipped C.O.D. It would take a week or ten days.

The Operative said she would like the machine immediately to clean her apartment. Mr. Leufer then said he had a bigger and better machine out in the car. She could have *that* right away. The Operative asked why she couldn't clean up her apartment with the little machine? But Mr. Leufer was already dashing out to his car to get the bigger machine. This one, he explained when he came back, cost a bit more: $200, in fact. He showed her how beautifully it worked.

The Operative said she would prefer to have the little $12.95 machine, if it was all right with him.

"Well," said Mr. Leufer, "when I told you this big machine was worth $200—it isn't really. Actually, it's only $169.50. However, there's a special on right now, and you can have it for $149.95."

Operative 67 said she wanted the little machine.

Mr. Leufer, battling manfully, offered to throw in a box of flatware free if she would consent to buy the big one. The Operative refused. Mr. Leufer offered to sell the flatware to another customer for $20 so that she might have the machine for a mere $129.95.

The Operative said she wanted the little machine.

Mr. Leufer gamely replied that he would let her steal the big machine from him for $109.95 cash. He said he would claim it had a scratch on it; he would tell the company he was selling it as a demonstrator. "Sorry," said the Operative, "the little machine, please."

Mr. Leufer began to attack the little machine. He pointed out that it had no filter to catch the dirt that sifted through the bag. He explained that the motor was not sealed, as it would be in a high-quality machine. He warned the Operative it would have to be serviced at least three or four times a year; the dust was forever getting into the grease on the bearings. Not only that, he declared—she could not operate the machine for more than twelve minutes at a time because the case tended to overheat.

"I don't care," said the Operative doggedly. "I still want it."

Wearily, Mr. Leufer brought out a contract for the Operative to sign. The document stated that she had received and paid for a machine at $12.95. Mr. Leufer explained, however, that she would not actually receive the machine for some days because the one he had with him was a demonstrator. Her machine would be sent C.O.D.

No money had changed hands, and Operative 67 still had no machine, but President Electric had a contract (in quadruplicate) in which she acknowledged that she had bought one. Mr. Leufer went away with his big machine, and the Operative reported that he was just a little bit annoyed.

Twelve days later the Operative phoned President Electric Ltd. to ask where her vacuum cleaner was. It took some time to reach the right man, and he tried to explain to her what a fool she was to buy the little machine (which is called the Ideal) instead of the big machine (the President).

"Why, for the time you would use the President you'll

probably use up a dozen machines like the little Ideal. And by the time you add money to it in cleaning and oiling and service you'll spend *twice* as much as the President costs you. If something breaks on the Ideal, you have to pay for it yourself. If a hose breaks, you pay $5.50; the motor burns out—you pay $17. You've got to get it serviced at least twice a year—that costs $6. And in a year or so you'll be looking for another vacuum cleaner."

Operative 67 said she still wanted the $12.95 machine.

The man said the little machine was not strong enough to remove anything but surface dirt from a rug—it could not remove sand or grit or anything of that nature. The Operative said she didn't care: she wanted it.

The man on the phone said it would take some time for the machine to reach her. There might be trouble at the border, he explained; the machine came from Japan and there had been a delay in orders.

The days passed. The Operative phoned again and asked for her machine. This time she got a different man and a different story. He could not tell her when she would receive her machine. He would have to check with the shipping department. Unfortunately, the stockroom was closed. He really could not say when it would be open.

The Operative offered to come down to the office herself and personally pick up the machine and pay for it. The man on the phone said that would not be possible because the machines were shipped directly from the manufacturer. "Don't worry," the man said, "we'll ship you the machine just as soon as we can."

But they did not ship it until I reported this extraordinary case in my column. Then, quite suddenly, it arrived. It was, the Operative reported, a good little machine. I am told, however, that any salesman who lets one out of his clutches is subject to instant dismissal.

3

On another memorable occasion I suggested to the Operative that she consider investing $2,500 in a great business venture. We were both intrigued by a certain advertisement which had a fey quality all its own. But after a lengthy investigation the Operative reported that she would not care to sink a nickel in the idea.

The advertisement which caught our eye read:

WHAT IS A PIXIE CENTER?
If you have $2,500 available for investment purposes and are of good character, whether male or female, write for details. Box 2780 Star. Please include phone number.

The Operative received a prompt answer to her letter of inquiry. A Mr. Charles Wilkinson called to say that he could tell her nothing over the phone; he would need an appointment to speak to her in person. And the following morning he arrived in his shiny white Cadillac, announcing that he had nothing whatsoever to sell. (The Operative has come to realize that when men in Cadillacs arrive at the door announcing they have nothing to sell, they usually have the Brooklyn Bridge or its equivalent, marked down, in the trunk.)

The Operative has run across some pretty preposterous business deals in her day, but this one, was, to use her expression, "the living end."

Mr. Wilkinson, suave and well-groomed, explained that Pixie Salons Limited was looking for "members" and that, if the Operative would fill in an Application for Membership, the board would consider it carefully. She might, for the modest investment of $2,500 and a few hours' work a week, make at least $800 a month.

He explained the *modus operandi:* Pixie Salons Limited manufactured a line of coin-operated weight-reducing machines. These machines were installed in beauty salons across Canada. The "members" picked up the cash from these machines once a week, at closing time. The company could not afford to employ people in every town of the land just to collect money once a week; that is why it had worked out the member system. They were looking for honest people, said the smooth-talking Mr. Wilkinson.

The equipment, he added, was worth $5,000; Pixie was prepared to invest half of that money and the member would become a partner by investing the other half.

The servicing operations, as he outlined them, seemed childishly simple. Once a week the honest Pixie member was to visit the beauty salon where the machines were installed and remove the money. He was to give twenty-five per cent of this to the owner of the beauty salon and keep the remainder, save for fifteen per cent, which he would send to the company. In this way, Mr. Wilkinson said, a member could get his or her investment back in three or four months. The company would not get its investment back for a couple of years, but it was willing to wait.

What a kind, generous bunch of business tycoons! thought Operative 67. *Not at all like the kind we see portrayed in the proletarian press. And so trusting, too! Why, these people are quite willing to accept my word that the money I send them every week represents fifteen per cent of the take! You could steal them blind, if you were the thieving type.*

Mr. Wilkinson next produced a member's "Application Form," which deserves to be framed as an example of the kind of business document that only a guaranteed genuine nickel-plated sucker would ever put his name to.

The "Application" was, in fact, a binding agreement to purchase equipment from Pixie Salons Limited for $5,000.

At the top of the order were these words: "Please accept

my order for the complete 'Pixie Package.'" It was Mr. Wilkinson himself who said that the figure $5,000 would have to be inserted since that was the total amount of the investment. Naturally, he added, he would write in that the company was paying half. The Operative could not understand this complication. Why didn't he just write in $2,500 and let it go at that? It seemed to her that if he wrote in $5,000 and she signed the document, then she would be liable for $5,000.

This was especially true since, in much smaller print at the very end of the document, she found that interesting clause which so many people pass over. This clause explained that the purchase agreement was complete in itself, that it could not be rescinded, that it contained *all* the terms of the agreement between the signator and Pixie Salons, that anything said verbally did not count, and that the only thing that *did* count was what was printed on the form.

Another interesting aspect of this purchase agreement was that the Operative would have no idea whatsoever what she was purchasing. Only after the entire sum was paid did the company agree to supply and install the equipment listed in "Schedule A."

But, oddly, there was no "Schedule A." When the Operative innocently asked about it, Mr. Wilkinson explained that he did not have a copy since at this point Schedule A did not exist.

Mr. Wilkinson appeared slightly annoyed. Nobody had ever asked about that before, he said. After all, this was only an application; it had not even been accepted. How, he asked, could his firm give the Operative a list of equipment and literature when it did not yet know which beauty salon the Operative would be assigned to and how much equipment would be needed?

When the Operative then asked to be shown a specific salon, Mr. Wilkinson was thunderstruck. He indicated that this kind of curiosity was unknown among prospective members of the great Pixie family.

As a matter of fact, there were a couple of further items that bothered the Operative. Not only did this neat little agreement not list what it was she was buying, but it also did not mention any guaranteed date of delivery. Nor did it state where or what would be delivered to whom. All it stated was that she was committing herself to a considerable sum and that "if her application was accepted" she could not wriggle out of it. She refused to sign, even when Mr. Wilkinson, his back to the wall, offered to accept the application, produce a Schedule A, and show her a real beauty center.

Pixie Salons Limited, it developed, had come into operation about eight months before. Since that time the asking price had gone up and down like an elevator. In August it was $4,000, in November $2,000, in March $2,500. Mr. Wilkinson was vice-president of the company, and he and the president, Paul Saunders, turned out to be old hands at this kind of franchise sale. Mr. Saunders was president of Continental Fire Services, which sold franchises on fire-alarm systems. Mr. Wilkinson was formerly connected with Infra Pac Systems, which sold franchises for machines which keep sandwiches hot, as described in the previous chapter.

Such schemes are usually advertised as "money-making opportunities," and they often are—for businessmen of the caliber of Mr. Saunders and the Cadillac-driving Mr. Wilkinson.

4

Then there was the time Operative 67 tried to get the Vitasafe Company to sue her. She tried for more than a year, but again she met with frustration.

Vitasafe, which is in the mail-order vitamin business in a big way, has an ingenious method of forcing its product on the consuming public. It showers prospective customers by mail, then gets tough if they don't pay. As all this starts with a "free trial offer," no strings attached, there is no legal basis for action. Nonetheless, thousands have been bamboozled by lawyers' letters and garnishee threats into paying for pills they do not want and have not used. The Operative got all these threats but, oddly, she could get no one to sue her.

I asked three people to answer the Vitasafe advertisements over a period of a year. Each tore out a coupon which read: *Send me free 30-day supply of Vitasafe Capsules as checked below,* and sent it to the address in the ad. By return mail each received a letter which explained that the thirty-day supply was "yours to try absolutely free . . . there were *no* strings attached." The letter went on to say: "If you are completely satisfied . . . you will then be given the opportunity of deciding whether or not you wish to continue as a member of the Vitasafe plan so you can receive a number of vitamins and minerals you may need every month as regular as clockwork. . . . If for any reason you should not want to receive the additional vitamins, simply let us know and that will end the matter."

The ingenious thing about this scheme is that the onus was placed on the prospect to tell the company he did not want to buy. A similar device is used by various mail-order stamp dealers in the United States who advertise "free" stamp offers to small boys, send packages of stamps "on approval" with the free ones, and then threaten legal action if the boys do not pay up.

My three operatives decided to see what would happen if they simply threw away the vitamins and ignored the Vitasafe Company entirely. Over the months they each received a total of nine form letters—each letter growing progressively more threatening.

The first letter was an invoice (the amounts varied between $8 and $12), to which was appended a polite note: "*Honestly*, do you feel there is something wrong with this statement? It hasn't received your attention and we would like to hear *your* side of the story."

The next form letter was equally charming: "This is a friendly reminder. Your account is overdue. Won't you please mail your remittance today?"

The third letter had a slight edge on it: "One of the greatest compliments a person can receive is that of being completely trusted by a stranger. However, there is hardly anything more disappointing than to have one's trust in a fellow misplaced. Several months ago we were that stranger who trusted you. . . ." The letter went on to say: "We simply cannot wait for payment any longer" and "we must therefore insist that you sit right down before the matter slips your mind again and send us your payment without further delay."

The next form letter came from "the chairman of the financial planning committee": "We hate as a rule to get excited about such a relatively small amount. And I, personally, dislike the usual 'collection letter' which burdens the reader with internal problems of our organization or which 'calls for law.' The trouble, however, is. . . ."

The next letter dropped the "dear friend" salutation: "Please take note: We have already allowed your debt to us to be left unpaid for much longer than is customary. We don't like to make a peremptory demand for payment but you appear to be wilfully forcing us to do so. Unless you send us your remittance in 10 days you will compel us to take drastic action."

One month later (in each case) a letter arrived marked: "FINAL NOTICE BEFORE LEGAL ACTION": "You leave us no alternative: We must surrender your account to our lawyers for collection. Apparently you do not realize the position in which you have placed yourself by disregarding your obligation to us," etc. etc. The letter urged that payment be made in ten days: "Use airmail, special delivery—even wire if necessary. . . ."

It was another month before the next form letter arrived, undated and not personally signed. This was from B. Weinstein, Barrister. "My client has requested me to promptly institute legal proceedings against you to have you pay this debt together with all expenses incurred for its collection. I am, therefore, preparing instructions to my agent solicitor whose office is in your community to commence legal proceedings against you. Such procedure can only result in additional expense and embarrassment to you. . . . My client informs me that you ordered a sample shipment from him and agreed to accept and pay for further shipments on a monthly basis until you notified him to the contrary. He insists that this is a just debt which he is determined to collect. . . ."

Operative 67, who enjoys talking to lawyers, tried to get Mr. Weinstein on the phone but was only able to reach his secretary. Mr. Weinstein, no doubt, was closeted with one of his vast network of agent solicitors. The Operative asked the secretary when she was to be sued. The secretary said she didn't know. The Operative said that she was really anxious to be sued. The secretary sounded baffled and said she would have to check with Mr. Weinstein. The Operative phoned a couple of days later and said she would be happy to drop into the Weinstein office and pick up the legal papers. The girl on the phone said, in a confused tone, that that would not be possible.

This did not stop two more final notices from arriving. The first was a FINAL NOTICE (in red) from the Allied Collection Agencies, announcing a court action in seven days.

There was no court action. A month later another notice from the same collection agency cried out in large print: "Commencement of legal action that may result in GARNISHEE PROCEEDINGS at your place of employment will be recommended unless payment reaches our office within seven days."

Apparently nobody recommended legal action because nothing further happened. Operative 67, who is very persistent, kept on trying to reach Mr. Weinstein and to plead with him to sue her. As she had never agreed "to accept and pay for further shipments on a monthly basis" from Vitasafe, she felt she had an iron-clad case in court. The girl in Mr. Weinstein's office said that this sort of thing had never happened before. She sounded more than a little flustered.

5

The Operative's attempts to become a Family Counsellor and thus earn a guaranteed income plus bonus also met with frustration. It came about as a result of the following advertisement.

PART TIME DAY OR EVENING

MEN or women desirous of earning extra income, age no barrier. Experience unnecessary as training provided. Guaranteed income based on evening's work, plus bonus. APPLY to Family Counsellor Division of E. L. Webb and Associates. Suite 205, 3130 Bathurst St. for interview or phone Mr. James, 9 a.m.–5 p.m. for appointment

---

At my suggestion the Operative phoned the Family Counsellor Division of E. L. Webb and Associates to discover what the part-time work was. She returned with the following report:

* She did not meet a Mr. James, and there was no mention of E. L. Webb and Associates.

* She met a Mr. Smith, and he was connected with an organization called Archmount Memorial Services.

* Mr. Smith wanted the Operative to become a "counsellor," i.e., a salesman for Archmount, and sell "prearrangement" plans for $556.

* But before the Operative could become a counsellor, it developed the Operative would have to lay out $556 of her own money. This the Operative declined to do.

And what did the Archmount customer get for his $556? Well, *he* didn't get anything, but when he died his heirs were to get the $556 in cash. In lieu of interest they were also to receive a lovely plastic "vaultorium," or casket cover, and a handsome bronze placque to put on the customer's grave. But $556 was to pay for funeral expenses.

Actually, under the Archmount system, the customer paid for the plan by installments at $24 down and $12 a month for four years. Thus he actually paid a total of $604.

This did not seem a very good deal to the bewildered Operative, but people appeared to be signing up for it. At least Mr. Smith solemnly declared that he had made $1,000 in commissions during the first three weeks of the plan.

But, then, Mr. Smith's technique was not really to sell the advantages of what he called "prearrangement"; it was to sell the advantages of selling *other* people on the idea.

The Operative was told that for every plan she sold she would get $55.50 commission. Moreover, said Mr. Smith, most couples would want to buy a double plan for $1,112 ($111 commission) since the plan was not transferable: in other words, if a wife signed for it and her husband died first, she couldn't collect.

Then Mr. Smith began to show the Operative how she

could make real profits by turning her customers into sales-men. She would collect "override commissions" on these once-removed sales and so would make big money.

"Let's assume," said Mr. Smith, "that you get five people to buy the prearrangement plan, and each of those five get five more people. Now, say that each of these people sells a double. Why, you'd make $1,350 in commissions!"

All of this had a familiar ring to Operative 67, who re-membered the Nutri-Bio meetings she had attended on my behalf. She declined to pay the $16.84 which Mr. Smith wanted for a promotion kit. However, I was able to obtain one for myself, and a careful study of it revealed a remark-able thing. Except for certain passages which dealt with pre-arranged funerals instead of food products, the Archmount Memorial Services story was exactly the same as the Nutri-Bio story, word for word.

The Archmount Sales Manual was titled: "The Archmount Open Door to a Brighter, Happier and More Successful Present and Future." The Nutri-Bio Sales Manual was titled: "The Nutri-Bio Open Door to a Brighter, Happier and More Successful Present and Future."

Charles W. Young, president of Nutri-Bio, wrote:

I joined the Nutri-Bio family because I saw the possi-bilities of accomplishing everything my wife Ellen and I had ever wished. It was wonderful, rewarding work in which we had the opportunity of growing just as rapidly as we wanted to grow. I wish I could describe what our Nutri-Bio experience has meant to us. And—to us, more growth and happiness is ahead with all of us working to-gether.

Wrote Wesley Chowen, President of Archmount:

I joined the Archmount family because I saw the possi-bilities of accomplishing everything for which my wife

Audrey and I had ever wished. It was wonderful, rewarding work in which we had the opportunity of growing just
as rapidly as we wanted to grow. I wish I could describe
what our Archmount experience has meant to us. And—to
us, more growth and happiness is ahead with all of us
working together.

Chowen later wrote: "There is something quite different
about Archmount. You will recognize that difference as you
progress throughout the book." It was not so very different
since those exact words also appeared in the Nutri-Bio sales
manual.

Like Nutri-Bio, Archmount claimed to have sales aids, in
the form of films and records, to help its counsellors tell their
story. The film was described in about nine hundred words
and the description was identical to that of the Nutri-Bio
film. "It is wonderfully done and, in the estimation of experts,
the pacing is the finest which has ever been written in a
Sound Slide film presentation," wrote the Archmount company about its film. That is exactly what Nutri-Bio said about
its film. I expected both of them to be up for Academy
Awards the following spring.

There were some seventy closely typed manuscript pages
in the Archmount Sales Manual, and the wording slavishly
followed that of Nutri-Bio except in those instances where
some difference was necessary because of the nature of the
products and their price structure. Indeed, Archmount had
even borrowed some of Nutri-Bio's illustrations.

The Operative was forced to conclude that, attractive as
the proposition might be, she just did not have the stamina
to handle the job of Family Counsellor. If you can take $604
from a man over a four-year period simply by promising to
pay his survivors $556 (plus casket cover and placque), then
you are indeed a Houdini among counsellors.

8

The Gospel According to Arthur Murray

In July 1960 the U.S. Federal Trade Commission issued a cease and desist order against Arthur Murray, Inc., the licensor of 450 franchised dance studios, barring them from making bogus offers designed "to lure the innocent" into signing up for dance lessons. Thus the childishly simple "contests," the telephone quizzes, the crossword and zodiac puzzles vanished from the scene. The free dancing lesson, however, remains. It is no longer a prize in a contest, but it is still handed out to thousands of prospective students—to teen-agers, young matrons, businessmen, wheelchair cases, grandmothers, even occasionally to a corpse. The free lesson is the rock on which the vast Arthur Murray operation rests. Since the Murray salesmen (or "analysts," as they prefer to be called) cannot put a foot in the prospect's door, their energies must be spent in luring the prospect's foot across *their* threshold. The free lesson is the bait—as valuable to the Arthur Murray network as the free brush is to the Fuller Brush Company.

Anyone who accepts a free lesson from Arthur Murray (or "$35 worth of free lessons," as the telephone salesgirls phrase it) can expect to find himself the unwitting object of a subtle and fiendishly effective psychological campaign designed to sign him up for dozens, scores, hundreds—even thousands of hours of dancing. Court records across the United States and Canada are sprinkled with the complaints of men and women who finally awoke to the unpalatable truth that they had committed great chunks of their savings to learn to dance mambo, samba, and cha-cha.

There is the case of William Willsea, a blind cigar vendor from Yonkers, who paid some $9,000 to a Murray studio for dancing lessons. There is the case of Mrs. Mary Bossung, of St. Louis, who paid $10,000. There is the case of Mrs. Gladys Brahm, a Florida widow, who paid the St. Petersburg studio $17,522. There is the case of Mrs. Gladys Foss, of St. Louis, who shelled out $20,501—just to learn to dance. Finally there is the case of Howard Lyons, of Calgary, a shy bachelor of forty-nine, who squandered at the local Murray studio a legacy of $51,000: $36,000 for dancing lessons and $15,-000 in the form of a loan to the studio.

Why should anybody pay $36,000 just to learn to dance? Two answers were given in the case of Howard Lyons, and there was truth in both of them.

A former backer of the studio put it this way: "Mr. Lyons is a prestige member of the studio and highly regarded by other members. He bought himself a place in the world."

The judge who handled the suit that Lyons brought against the studio put it another way. He said that Lyons was suffering from "mental infirmity arising from the exercise of undue influence and mesmerism" by the Arthur Murray studio. He declared Lyons incompetent to handle his own affairs—not because he was originally of unsound mind but only because of the current mesmerization.

Few of the lonely widows, insecure spinsters, desolate bachelors, and others who walk into the Murray studio clutching their free gift certificates comprehend the extent to which they will be brainwashed over the coming weeks. In the Arthur Murray scheme of things, little is left to chance. Every employee the student encounters—from the girl who takes her name, the dazzling young "analyst" who teaches the opening steps, the regular teacher who befriends her, right up to the manager, the supervisor, and finally Arthur Murray himself—is working to a careful script, the words of which have been memorized and the gestures rehearsed in daily sales conferences. From the instant he or she walks in the door, the affluent student becomes the object of a carefully contrived campaign whose ultimate goal is to sell the equivalent of a lifetime of dancing lessons, the cost of which can be as high as $12,000. Each step of this campaign is laid out in pamphlet form as specifically as the steps of the rumba or tango.

Although the techniques and prices sometimes vary from studio to studio and season to season, the basis is generally the same. The student is made to want a lifetime of dancing lessons so badly that, in the end, he will eventually go down on his knees pleading to be allowed to spend a small fortune. For Arthur Murray is not selling just dancing lessons; he is selling something far more basic. He is selling confidence, friendship, social status, prestige, surcease from loneliness. For thousands of people, the world literally revolves around a Murray studio. It is their anchor in life and they will sacrifice a new car or a summer vacation, sell their bonds and

securities, forgo other worldly pleasures to achieve what to
them is the most important thing in the world, all the more
tantalizing because it will be made to seem virtually unattainable. The significant thing about the Murray organization is not that there have been damage suits against it by
former students but, considering the size of the enterprise
and the sums obtained, that these suits have been relatively
few in number. Scores have paid their $5,000 or their $8,000
or their $12,000, or even more, without a murmur or a back-
ward glance. Like the mesmerized Howard Lyons, they buy
themselves a place in the world, and even if that world is an
artificial one they are content. In Toronto there is one
middle-aged widow who has purchased *four* lifetime courses
from Arthur Murray for an amount estimated at $36,000. She
has not complained. After all, did the studio not name a
ballroom in her honor and put her picture in it?

2

The step-by-step process by which a young girl is persuaded
to commit herself to several hundred dollars' worth of dancing lessons can be examined through a manual issued some
years ago by Louise Taylor, manager of Arthur Murray's
San Francisco studio. The techniques described here change
in detail, of course, depending on the studio and the personnel involved; and there have been some refinements since
the manual was issued, for all the Murray techniques are
constantly being polished and improved; the basic psychology, however, is unchanged.

Let us suppose in this case that the prospect strolls into
the studio to inquire about the price of a course. This she

will certainly not be given. Instead she will be greeted by the registrar, who will explain the Murray System and then check the prospect's dancing style.

It is the registrar's job to turn over a work sheet and suggested "plan," containing his comments, to the "dance analyst," with whom the pupil quickly comes into contact. These comments are really for the prospect's benefit—to convince her that she can be a wonderful dancer and to suggest subtly that it is not easy to get more lessons from Arthur Murray.

The registrar is saved the taxing mental problem of composing these comments. Samples of what to write are given to him in the manual under *Remarks:*

> *Mr. Dance Analyst:* Miss Pupil has never danced before but on our first analysis hour she showed excellent possibilities. She has missed too much fun—so work hard to give her the confidence and relaxation she needs. If enough progress is shown, perhaps we can plan a more extensive course for Mr. Head Registrar's approval. Good Luck!

This last sentence leaves the door ajar for a further sale of dancing lessons to the prospect.

The registrar is also given a series of "comments" to scrawl across the work sheet. Sample: *Two-dance course. Hope more extensive course will be approved by Mr. Head Registrar.*

The registrar is then instructed to tell the prospect that "the only way you can take more lessons is if the Dance Analyst submits a qualified plan that is approved. Do well in your first few hours so that approval is possible. It will take extra effort on your part but we should like to have you with us as long as possible."

Out floats Miss Pupil into the arms of Mr. Dance Analyst, as the Arthur Murray manual calls him. These analysts, male and female, are key personnel in the Murray System. They are usually with the new pupil for five lessons only. In that time it is their task to learn everything they can about the new arrival: what kind of person she is, what her weaknesses are, what she is seeking out of life, and—highly important—the state of her finances.

Most important of all, the analyst's job is to discover the pupil's "X-factor." The X-factor is an invention of a Massachusetts motivational research firm, which has done work for many of the Murray studios, and it is the foundation block on which the Murray selling psychology is built. The San Francisco manual describes it as "the pupil's personality background and emotional needs for dancing lessons. If you know his problem, you direct your emotional selling more effectively."

"Emotional selling" is the other key phrase used in Arthur Murrayland. "Know emotional selling so well that you can convince the pupil he needs more lessons," each analyst is advised. "Build desire to overcome other needs (car, trip, etc.) or to make sacrifices of time. . . . Describe the course you are planning in flowing emotional terms. . . ."

In the classes which are held by the studio to develop analysts, the prospective salesmen practice the art of the pleasant greeting. "The first ten minutes are of paramount importance for a Dance Analyst. A smile upon meeting the prospect, and a sincere friendly attitude, can extend your 25 hours to 50 hours immediately." And so the opening greeting is carefully prescribed: *I'm Mr. Analyst. I've been looking forward to this lesson. Mr. Registrar told me how much he enjoyed teaching you.*

The analyst's first step is to take the new pupil into his or her confidence by sharing the private messages the registrar has inscribed on the work sheet and plan.

"Judging from the comment Mr. Registrar wrote me, you must really have done well on your trial lesson," he says. He opens the plan which the registrar has laid out and refers to the worksheet within: "I see you not only are qualified for a basic temporary course, but I'm to introduce you to *all* the dances." Now he looks back at the plan: "This is the comment I spoke to you of. I don't see why I shouldn't read it to you." And he reads what the registrar has written.

An "analysis lesson" follows. It is a sales talk to music. The analyst has memorized a series of "sentences that create desire," encouraging remarks that he feeds to the prospect as they move awkwardly about the floor.

You've learned so much; it's really rare to find someone who picks it up so quickly. . . . With your rhythm I think I shall be able to add Balboa to your course. . . . You are making such wonderful progress, I wish I could teach you your advanced course myself. . . .

The pupil has not only been flattered but has also been subtly reminded that (*a*) there is an advanced course and (*b*) this charming young man will not be her teacher for long.

After half an hour of dancing there is a three-minute break during which the dance analyst's instructions are to discover the pupil's X-factor. He has been trained to do this at a special class in which prospective dance analysts pair off— adopting the role of analyst and pupil—and practice conversational leads that will help them to determine the following essentials: Where did the pupil spend her early youth? Where did she go to school? Did she take part in social activities? What led her to her present location and vocation? Who are her friends? What does she do for fun?

The dancing lesson begins again and at the end of the

hour the analyst explains what his job is. He will work on all the dances with the pupil during the first few hours, analyzing her dancing and planning a course of lessons. Then she will be turned over to a regular teacher.

"Perhaps you won't need many more lessons than the course you are on," the helpful analyst is told to say, "but, if you have the ability, I'd like to plan a more extensive course for you."

Thus a seed is planted: if more dancing lessons are offered, it will be a flattering sign of the student's ability.

At the end of the lesson the analyst has a set of key phrases memorized which are designed to force the pupil to admit she has had a good time.

"I certainly enjoyed the lesson, didn't you?" he asks. Or: "We are going to have a good time, aren't we?" It's difficult for anybody but an out-and-out boor to answer anything but yes. (*Float her out of the studio on a wave of enthusiasm!* is the way the manual puts it.)

The second lesson begins with the usual warm, sincere, carefully manufactured greeting: "Are you as anxious to get started again as I am? I hope so. After you did so well on your first lesson, I told Mr. Registrar how happy I was that he picked me to be your first teacher."

Then the analyst drops the hint that only certain people can qualify at Arthur Murray's. The plan he is working on has to be approved by the dreaded approval committee. ("I had a plan disapproved once and I never want that to happen again," he is taught to say.) The approval committee's instructions are to fill out the pre-approval check sheet "after much deliberation," so that the pupil feels her progress is being carefully watched.

During the lessons, additional flattering "Sentences That Create Desire" pop from the analyst's mouth. ("With your unusual sense of balance, given a little more time, I can make you as good on the dance floor as you are on the golf course.")

The pupil is also introduced to other key pupils.

"I want you to meet Miss Keber. She is a wonderful person. You'll notice how confident she is. She was very shy when she first came in. I started her out, too. Dancing has seemed to give her a great deal of poise. She is very popular and always has a good time at our clubs and parties. Don't you think our studio has a warm atmosphere?" And, indeed, there *is* an air of warmth, enthusiasm, and "happiness" among the pupils who go dancing by.

Now the time has come to expand the pupil's horizons. "I don't want you to continue just concentrating on the two-dance course. That isn't sufficient for your ability. You can see that no one dance is independent of the other. That's why I'm anxious for you to qualify for the plan I'm preparing for you. . . ."

At this point the analyst is instructed to "insulate her against the shock of being sold a big course. Get her acclimated to the 300-hour atmosphere and the Lifetime will be easier."

So the analyst points out other pupils and lets the prospect know how many hours of dancing they are taking.

"I want you to watch Mr. Harding. When he first came in he couldn't dance a step. Now he has such confidence! He was very nervous when he took his preliminary exam but on his intermediate exam he was so poised you wouldn't have recognized him as the same person. He has completed nearly 125 hours of his 250-hour course. Isn't he doing well?" Again the pupil finds herself agreeing with the analyst. Without really realizing it, she is committing herself to the Arthur Murray way of life. Very shortly she will be in a mood to sign a conditional sales contract for far more dancing lessons than she originally expected to take.

3

It is all but impossible for anybody to walk in off the street and find out how much a dancing lesson at Arthur Murray's costs. That is because you cannot buy a single lesson under the Murray system. Nor can you learn a single dance —the cha-cha, for instance. You buy lessons in bulk and learn all the dances.

Operative 67, whom I asked to investigate the Toronto studio, was told at the end of her first free lesson that Arthur Murray had several dancing courses at various prices. Her analyst, a beautifully groomed and diamond-ringed young man, said the studio was not allowed to release a price list. However, he recommended a $15-a-week course in which eight dance steps were learned. The total cost of this course came to $510 and entitled the pupil to thirty private lessons, thirty public lessons, and parties twice a week. (There was as much stress placed on this social life as on the dance lessons.)

When the Operative balked, the analyst unveiled a second course, with half as many lessons, for $276. Later he came up with a "baby basic offer" for $190 which entailed ten public and ten private lessons. He insisted that this was the cheapest available course, but when the Operative shook her head he managed to remember a special introductory plan, which, he said, his supervisor must approve.

An interesting charade followed. The supervisor appeared reluctant to approve the offer. The friendly analyst pleaded with him. The supervisor said he would have to get special permission from New York. "But she has such a good record!" exclaimed the analyst, bringing out his pink file. (My instructions to the Operative had been to dance as badly as possible.) The supervisor allowed himself to be persuaded.

He claimed that the course was worth $104 but said the Operative could have it for $84. The Operative claimed she had a $35 gift certificate, and this was also included, so that the basic price for five private and five public lessons came to $49 in cash.

The Operative was told that she must sign immediately. When she said she needed time to think the matter over, the supervisor grew angry. However, the analyst again took his pupil's part and whispered that he would calm his superior down. The offer was held open.

Later that week the Operative compared notes with a fellow student who had won a $25 gift certificate in a contest. The studio had told *her* that the same ten-lesson course cost $74. With the free certificate this also came to $49. This supports the generally held belief that dancing lessons at Murray studios average out at about five dollars each.

There is more than a suspicion, however, that higher rates are quoted to make the prospect believe he is going to get a bargain. The San Francisco manual contains a drill developed for students who have been awarded two free dancing lessons but have declined to enroll in the basic twenty-five-hour course. Here is the prescribed sales approach:

"Before your certificate expires today," the interviewer says, "we can arrange for you to continue with ten additional lessons, just like the two that you won, which will give us the time we need."

She then produces the enrollment agreement and says: "The standard rate for ten lessons is $75."

She writes that amount down to impress the prospect and then continues: "Mr. Murray has arranged a discount of about forty per cent for people like yourself who are his certificate guests. You may enroll today for only $48 instead of $75. The $27 discount is written off to his advertising account. . . ."

It is made quite clear to the prospect that he must sign at once if he is to take advantage of the discount. If backed right into a corner, however, the Murray salesmen in San Francisco were able to come up with a five-lesson course "as a last resort."

"The $48 is what's bothering you, isn't it? Now, here is what I am going to do for you. We will split this—you take one half, and I know another pupil just like you, who will be thrilled to pick up the other half. He has been waiting for this opportunity. You'll be doing him a favor as well as yourself. All right? How much do you want to pay as a deposit tonight?"

The manual makes clear that the main object is to get the pupil to sign a contract. "The important thing is to enroll the pupil. If pupil says he is concerned about both the down payment and the amount of the monthly payment, this admission is a commitment that he wants the course so both quotes must be reduced."

The amount of the down payment and the monthly payments is immaterial since, under the terms of the non-cancelable contract, the payments must be met regardless of whether or not the dancing lessons continue. If the pupil breaks a leg, falls sick, leaves town, or loses interest, he still owes the money once his name goes on that legal document.

4

When a student commits himself to a course of dancing lessons at Arthur Murray's, he is really committing himself to a new way of life.

He does not pop in for his twice-weekly hour of instruction and pop out again like a man with a dental appointment; he quickly finds himself enmeshed in the web of the studio, which may easily occupy most of his spare waking hours. The studio becomes a kind of second home to him, a haven in an unfriendly world, where he is appreciated, flattered, and befriended. For many a middle-aged man or woman, the Arthur Murray studio fulfills the same comforting psychological role that the street-corner gang does for parentless youths; it is a place where you feel you belong.

It goes without saying that this approach is as carefully planned as everything else in the Murray empire, where there is a manual for every phase of development, an approved answer to every question, and a precedent written down for every hypothetical situation. A standard Murray sales-training ploy is the "mock situation" in which the teachers are handed hypothetical problems by their superiors and asked to act out the method they would use to deal with it. ("Mr. Jones is ready for his Bronze Medal, but he doesn't yet know he wants one. I'll be Mr. Jones. Now, you sell me.")

Trained psychologists are employed by the huge Toronto studio (one of the largest on the continent), and a motivational-research expert comes in once or twice a year and spends several days pepping up the teaching staff. "When he's finished with you, you feel like you've had a shot of dope," one Murray teacher told me. Dancing is not mentioned in these sessions, which are reserved for more subtle techniques.

One simple teacher-pupil relationship was so transparently cloying that some of the personnel winced when they heard it. It was, in fact, the old confidence-man approach reduced to its starkest essentials. Each teacher was instructed to go up to a pupil, sit down beside him, and say earnestly: "Don't be frightened. I want to be your friend. Do you want to be mine?" Cloying or not, those who used the technique found it to be electrifying in its effectiveness.

"By the time a teacher has had a student for fifteen or

thirty hours she even knows what time he brushes his teeth and what toothpaste he uses," the same Murray veteran told me. "By then your student will do anything for you. If you asked him to go out on the dance floor and stand on his head, he'd do it. He does it because he trusts you. You've shown interest in him and he's pathetically grateful."

As in the case of the con man–Egg relationship, the attitude is not exactly one of romance—but of trust based on flattery. "It's not so much puppy love as an indebtedness to the teacher," I have been told. "They're pathetically grateful that anyone would do so much for them." Again, the classic parallel of the seduction springs to mind. The teacher lets the student see, through her, the flattering image he wants to project of himself. When that image is accepted, the bond is complete.[1]

A student in Arthur Murrayland is never happier than when he is asked to participate in one of the scores of functions which keep the studio in a whirl of social activity. He will make sandwiches until his arms ache, dress up in costume, help decorate the studio, and—most important—actually sell dancing lessons, all in the interests of belonging to the In-Group.

A potent sales tool used on beginners is the calendar of social events. It indicates that something exciting is going on almost every evening at Arthur Murray's. An air of constant frenzy permeates the premises and, though much of it is manufactured, a good deal of it is genuine. The enthusiasm is infectious, and the staff itself is caught up in it, so that when the peak is reached during the mad six-week circus known as the Dancers' Derby, the teachers themselves are as mesmerized as the students.

[1] Some students do, of course, fall in love with their teachers, and this is a continuing source of worry to the Murray organization, which tries to keep it to a minimum by forbidding all out-of-studio fraternization by staff members on pain of instant dismissal.

The Dancers' Derby is the climax of the Arthur Murray year, and it is a little like Christmas every day. It is, in actuality, an intensive six-week sales period, but it is billed as an exciting contest with prizes for almost everybody. During this period a studio may easily sell as many dancing lessons as it would during the rest of the year. In the final hectic day of the 1957 Derby, for instance, the Toronto studio sold $87,000 worth.

Teachers and students alike are conditioned to the frenzy of the Derby by a series of lesser events that seem to be almost unending. These run all the way from the birthday parties (standard for every student) to the gigantic Medal Balls, which take place three times a year.

There are the Match Competitions, in which students and studios compete for dancing excellence. (To score top points the competitors find they must sign up for extra lessons.)

There are the Student Recitals, in which a student is given the use of a room to demonstrate his dancing skill to friends, who are given a free lesson as a reward for attending. (Almost without realizing it, the student has become an Arthur Murray salesman.)

The Medal Balls are prestige affairs to honor those students who have been awarded a bronze, silver, or gold medal, in ascending order of dancing excellence. Preceding these Medal Balls, the excitement builds to a pitch as each student crams more and more dancing hours into the week in order to be able to qualify for the coveted prize.

Before the ball, each student qualifying for a medal must pass a dance examination. By this time he is obsessed with the idea that he may fail. He sweats and sometimes faints dead away, so great is the emotion of the moment. In Toronto I have been told of prominent barristers, judges, professors, and businessmen entering the sacred precincts of the dance board with their hands clammy, their faces chalk white, and their knees knocking so hard it was almost impossible for them to dance at all. Yet few actually fail.

At the Medal Balls, the medalists themselves provide the floor show, each demonstrating his skill to thunderous applause. During the week that follows—Medal Pageant Week—the medalists are treated like foreign potentates. They float in a kind of dream through the studio, wearing their medals and accepting the praises of the multitude. Their teachers, too, are caught up in this orgy of hosannas, and it is not unknown for teachers to break down and cry with their pupils when a medal is presented. The tears and smiles are encouraged specifically in the Murray manuals but are often genuine enough. Just as each student desperately seeks the regard of his teacher, so each teacher desires the esteem of his supervisor—and so on up the long ladder past manager, franchise owner, and regional director to that cloud-flecked throne where Arthur Murray himself is seated—a stern, yet kindly, forbearing, and all-wise God-figure.

Is it necessary to add that, during Medal Pageant Week, a special effort is made to sign up more students? Dazzled by the halos shining above each medalist and enticed by a special twenty per cent discount for cash, the lesser students rush to add more lessons to their schedules in the hope that, when another four months roll around, they, too, may achieve the ranks of the anointed.

Apart from the great carnival of the Derby, the biggest day of the year at Arthur Murrayland is "A" Day, or Approval Day. This is the day when students are "approved" in large batches for bigger and better dancing courses. The key word here is "approved," which has the same significance in Arthur Murray's lexicon as "qualify" has in the encyclopaedia salesman's. The emphasis is on exclusiveness, but the dance board, which seems to deliberate so carefully, rarely refuses to allow the eager applicant to move up the ladder.

Grade A "closers," strangers to the students, are brought in from New York to ease the signatures onto the new and more expensive contracts. One bit of byplay practiced in Toronto prevented the studio from losing face if it developed that the student really did not wish to take more lessons. When this awful fact became obvious, it was the practice of the supervisor to grow angry and rip up the chart on which the teacher had plotted the student's future.

"How dare you bring this pupil in?" the supervisor would cry, eyes flashing. "Can't you see he's not ready!"

This so angered one student that he signed up for a more expensive course, out of pique. The technique is known within the organization as "fear selling."

The Annual Dancers' Derby concentrates all the Arthur Murray sales techniques into a single six-week period. Every one of the familiar big-sell tricks is used here—the something-for-nothing psychology of the Big Prize Contest; the sympathy approach of the point-collecting magazine salesman; the you-be-a-salesman technique of the water-softener men; the subtle flattery of the song sharks. During the Derby the spirit of free competition, which distinguishes Western society, seems to be twisted to the point of ultimate lunacy. Student competes with student, teacher with teacher, supervisor with supervisor, studio with studio. Here the student's loyalty to his teacher and to his studio becomes a form of unalloyed patriotism of the kind that is generally seen only during the crisis of war.

Winning points in the great Arthur Murray Derby suddenly becomes the most important thing in the world; nothing else matters. And somewhere along the way everyone seems to forget—even those who stand to profit from it—that every point represents one cash-sales dollar.

The Dancers' Derby is based on a point system. Teachers

and supervisors are awarded one point each for every cash dollar they bring into their studio during the six weeks, and half a point for each "paper" dollar, i.e., each financed dollar. Those with the most points win prizes, which increase sharply in value (a mink coat, a trip to Europe) if the studio itself, by virtue of a huge aggregate of points, wins out over competing studios of the same size. Before the Derby is over, so great is the excitement that the contestants are competing less for material things than simply for the sake of winning; for the winner gets far more than mink— he or she gains the plaudits of peers and superiors.

The students also get points—for signing up for further lessons or for bringing in new students. Thus, during the Derby everybody in the studio is a salesman. There are prizes for students, too, but these are less important to them than the idea that their team, or their teacher or their supervisor or their studio, should be the grand winner.

One former teacher remembers the odd spectacle of two middle-aged women students arguing bitterly—almost to the hair-pulling stage—about the relative prospects of their supervisors in the Derby.

"Mine is sure to get it!" cried one emphatically.

"She hasn't got a chance! She'll never get it. I tell you my supervisor is way ahead," cried the other, almost in tears.

So great was the excitement in Toronto one year that a woman student purchased two Lifetime memberships, at $12,000 each, to put the studio over the top as the biggest money-maker on the continent.

On another memorable day a supervisor, by dint of driving furiously around the city and pleading with her students, was able to sell an extra $17,000 worth of dancing lessons, simply because the students wanted her to win.

During the Derby, dancing lessons come to a near stand-still. There is little time for instruction. Sales replace terpsichore. Each week of the six-week period is given a different theme, but every theme bears on the main object—to sell more dancing lessons.

So great is the urge to compete, so all-encompassing the desire to win, that entire studios have become bemused to the point of near-insolvency, giving away so much that, in winning, they actually lose.

By the final week everyone is caught up in the frenzy. Arthur Murray himself has been phoning regularly. Charts show the daily position of each student, each teacher, each studio. Students will stay up until 4 a.m. to redecorate the hall in preparation for the Victory Party which is held no matter who wins.

"It isn't the money by this time," one teacher told me. "It's something more. It's prestige, I guess. You just have to beat the next guy. You want to show your students, who are a part of you now, that you're better than the other teachers. And you want to show your bosses, too. If the students are mesmerized, so are the teachers. We couldn't help it. Everybody at our place was mesmerized, including the owners themselves."

And perhaps, she might have added, even Mr. Arthur Murray.

5

There is one phrase that sends shivers down the spines of enthusiastic Arthur Murray staff members. The words: "I'll think it over" are anathema to them. However, each has memorized a variety of arguments with which to bedevil and sensitize procrastinators, and prevent hot prospects from cooling off. Thus, if a man stammers: "I'll think it over," his teacher is prepared to answer:

"No, Mr. Pupil, that won't solve anything. You have thought about it long enough. There isn't any point in your going around in a mental circle. The only thing that bothers you is money, isn't that right? Now, Mr. Pupil, this isn't something to put off and treat lightly. As a matter of fact, this will change your life, like buying a fur coat or taking a trip to Europe or getting married or buying a car. Now, you'd think nothing of putting $2,000 or $3,000 in a car. Good dancing is a vehicle; it will carry you on the road to happiness. Many wonderful exciting things are bound to happen to you—waiting just around the corner—people you will meet . . . things you will do. . . ."

The Murray sales staff is expert at meeting every possible objection a pupil can make at any stage of the course. However the prospect may boggle, he will be subjected to a careful counterattack of prepared arguments.[2] "Don't try to avoid objections," Murray sales personnel are told. "Learn to anticipate them. Learn to overcome them."

"We more or less shame them into a desire to dance," one former Arthur Murray instructor has been quoted as saying.

If a girl pupil says: "I don't want to be an expert, I just want to dance well enough to get by," her teacher may have this answer memorized:

I can't believe a statement like that. You have too much "on the ball" to be content with second-rate ambitions. Now look, would you, if you had the choice, prefer a plain unattractive man to a handsome man? Of course not. Would you prefer sitting at home instead of being at a

[2] The Toronto studio had mimeographed sheets of replies to objections from various studios in the United States.

gay party with a nice group of friends? No, you wouldn't.
. . . Dancing is insurance for good times all the rest of
your life. Now I don't mean to sound forceful, but you
see it makes me a little anxious for you when I think that
a woman of your caliber entertains the idea of "just
getting by" when there is so much in life waiting for you.
Please, Miss Pupil, let me arrange for your new course
and have the approval test next week—you will be able to
chalk it up as one of the wisest decisions of your life.

Some Murray studios are not above changing a pupil's
whole life. If a pupil says she is moving to a new town where
there is no Arthur Murray studio, the teacher is taught to
tell her that he has "such wonderful plans for you," if she
could only stay in town a little longer: "I was just planning
on starting the most advanced stage of dancing—you are
almost ready, you know. It would have made you a very
confident person. It always seems a shame when a girl like
you is unable to finish a job that has gotten off to such a
good start. . . ."

"Gosh, you *can't* stop now," says the teacher, warming to
his task. "Can't you possibly make arrangements to stay over
a little longer? . . . You could be the best dancer in your
town—and you know what that means. Good dancers deserve the unusual amount of popularity they receive. Please
stay, Miss Pupil. . . ."

For a man who says: "I'll have to talk it over with my
wife," the teacher has a scornful answer, which she delivers
with a light laugh.

Oh, come now, Mr. Pupil, you look like a man that's
capable of making his own decisions. Supposing you did
ask your wife and she said no—would you be willing to
give up all the good times that are in store for you? Does
your wife ask you every time she buys a hat? Of course

not. She wears the hat and looks very stunning but you don't begrudge it—no, it makes you proud of her. . . . Well, Mr. Pupil, you're going to wear your dancing, *good or bad,* the rest of your life.

The teacher then suggests that the pupil keep the lessons a secret from his wife and surprise her with his new-found abilities at some later date. "Because of your strong lead, you can show her off, and all your friends will comment on what a swell couple you make. . . ."

"Don't you see, Mr. Pupil, there are some things we just have to decide for ourselves. . . ." It is a strong man who can resist the implications of that line.

Similar shame techniques have been developed for those who say they can afford no more lessons, who claim their friends will laugh at them or who insist that they don't *like* the cha-cha. (*"Miss Jones, isn't it true that anything we don't know we tend to shy away from and say we don't like?"*)

It is hard to escape the conclusion that most of Arthur Murray's students really want to be talked out of their objections. After all, each has entered the studio voluntarily. The Toronto studio has issued to its teachers a manual regarding objections, which begins with this shrewd, if ungrammatical, preamble:

A large proportion of our pupils are the type introvert that needs help in making up his mind. Actually, they want to take more lessons, yet instead of immediately making up their minds, they will present all kinds of excuses why they can't take more. This type of pupil wants convincing assurances that she is doing the right thing. She wants to feel justified that it isn't foolish and a waste of time. They suspect there is something to gain by taking more lessons, but because of natural fear of being "taken" they need to be assured that it is a wise decision and much is to be gained by renewing.

The pamphlet then lists sixty possible objections, with answers suitable to each. Armed with these answers, the teacher-salesmen who make up the Murray organization can move their pupils step by step up the long ladder of Dancing Achievement—from the basic course to the Intermediate Course to the Advanced Course (known, significantly, as the Social Standard Course); and then on to dizzier heights; to the bronze medal, the silver medal, and the gold medal until finally she reaches that Cloudland where only an honored few samba their way to eternal happiness. The glittering portals of the Arthur Murray Lifetime Club are there before her. Goaded by her teacher, she hammers her tiny fists upon them, pleading to be allowed the privilege of entering.

6

The new pupil at Arthur Murray's soon senses that some of her fellows are more than ordinary students. There is a hallowed air about them, which sets them apart. At first, she does not understand this aura; but before long the word seeps down to her: these are the Anointed—the members of the exclusive Arthur Murray Lifetime Club,[3] fated to dance

[3] Though the Lifetime Club still exists, its activities have been heavily curtailed in many studios, where it has been replaced by—or re-named— the Arthur Murray Hobby Club, a somewhat less ambitious endeavor. The change came about partly as the result of the bad publicity the studios were receiving for pushing Lifetime memberships. In October 1962 the attorney general of California moved to take action against the practice of selling a "lifetime" of dancing lessons. (A new California statute in 1961 had made it illegal for dance studios to sell more than $500 worth of lessons or more than a seven-year term.) The Hobby Club, which operates else-

forever, at any studio anywhere in the world as long as they all shall live. It is for them that special cocktail parties are held; for them that special dance parties are arranged at the leading hotels; for them that special tables are reserved at the night clubs. They are distinguished by the gold Lifetime pin or tie clip and the special membership card engraved in gold—and also by an indefinable sense of Belonging. There is something else about them, too; but the new pupil does not yet realize it: each of these Lifetime members has spent $12,000 or thereabouts to achieve his special status. Perhaps this, more than anything else, qualifies them for Lifetime membership. There are some rude critics of the Arthur Murray system who firmly believe it is the only qualification.

Although the Murray organization persists in the pleasant fiction that only a special kind of student is chosen for Lifetime membership, the literature and instruction given to the teaching staff suggest that it is really considered just another sale, albeit a whopping one. The Toronto studio, for instance, printed a 10,000-word manual detailing the Lifetime procedure step by step. It summarized the key philosophy in this way:

1. The teacher should make it so glamorous and desirable that the pupil wants it more than anything else in the world.
2. The teacher and Supervisor must work hand in hand in discussing everything that is to take place before and after each lesson. If this is done carefully and the teacher rehearses what they are going to say, Lifetime courses will be the easiest renewals ever made.

---

where, is confined to 600 hours of lessons. Apart from this, however, the sales technique is similar to that described here, being based on exclusiveness and desire.

3. The Supervisor should do no obvious selling—that
    is accomplished by telling the teacher exactly what
    to say and do each time.
4. Above all, never let a pupil refuse the nomination to
    the Manager. It should be disapproved by the
    Supervisor before it gets that far.

This last point is made again and again in Arthur Murrayland: "Never put yourself in a position so that the student
can turn down a Lifetime Membership. It's either approved
or disapproved and by all means disapprove it rather than
have them be able to say that they were asked to become
a member but turned it down."

An enthusiastic student with means is likely to be tagged
early as a potential Lifetime sale. She will not know this for
some time, but she will become aware of a marked increase in
enthusiasm about her. Other teachers will start to greet her
by name and praise her. She will be asked to help organize
studio parties and help new students get acquainted. There
is even a thank-you line in the manual for teachers to use
when this happens.

That was so nice of you to take Mrs. ——— under your
wing and make her feel at home, but then that's just like
you to want to help.

Slowly the student begins to feel part of an In-Group.
Without knowing it, she is being prepared for step three in
the Lifetime procedure, known as "Building Desire."

The student begins to hear references to the Lifetime Club
from her teacher: "Mrs. Fenstart was thrilled pink when she
was accepted into the Lifetime Club. She loves to dance and
that means she'll be taking lessons the rest of her life and
will always be up on the latest trend. It's a non-profit club
too, you know. Isn't that wonderful?" (The phrases "Isn't

that wonderful?" and "Isn't this fun?" are used over and over again in Arthur Murrayland. My Operative 67 told me that it was this incessant chant, more than anything else, that drove her from the studio. It is a kind of reaffirmation of faith in the system, like a prayer repeated over and over at an old-time camp meeting.)

The student begins also to hear of the special fun the Lifetime members are having. The teacher has rehearsed a few lines of dialogue for the purpose, which sound oddly like a TV commercial.

TEACHER: Man, oh man, did we have a good time Saturday night.

STUDENT: Did you go dancing?

TEACHER: We certainly did! The Lifetime Club had a party Saturday night and I've never had such a wonderful time. You know I've been invited to practically every one of the Lifetime Parties and each one is better than the last. Mrs. ——— who has been a member for ——— years said it's always like that. It's wonderful to have a club like that where everybody has a common goal (which is good dancing) and they put themselves out to make everyone else happy. Don't you agree?

The student agrees. More and more, as she dances on, she finds herself agreeing with her wonderful friend, the teacher.

"Did you hear the latest?" her teacher will ask her. (Another carefully rehearsed remark.) "Mrs. Crankshaw was approved for Lifetime membership. Isn't that wonderful? I'm so happy for her and you should have seen her and her teacher when they got the news that Mr. Murray approved it. They were laughing and crying and jumping up and down. In fact everybody joined in. I think that's wonderful. One of these days I'm going to find someone I'd be proud to recommend as my Lifetime Member. . . ."

The days that follow are spent in getting "commitments" from the student. She does not know she is committing herself when the teacher asks her casually whether she intends to dance for the rest of her life, or whether she likes the studio and the staff, but if she answers "yes"—and the questions are designed to force her to answer "yes"—then she is on the way. The key question, however, is this one:

What would you do if you knew that as of right this minute you could never come into Arthur Murray's again? Never have another lesson?

The answer to this question determines that the student is ready to be guided into the all-important fourth step, which is designed to get a written commitment from her. She must write down in her own hand the tenets of her new faith.

"I have a terrific surprise for you," the teacher tells her after some preamble. "It's been on my mind for a few weeks, but I wanted to do a lot of research before I mentioned it to you. I'm still not completely sure. I know how I feel about you and I think I know how you would answer these things, but I have to hear it from you. . . ."

Then come the "qualifying questions" designed to get further verbal commitments from the student that Murrayland is Nirvana.

"I knew you'd say exactly that," the teacher says, "because I couldn't feel so strongly about something and have you feel any other way. When you just can't sleep over something and you are thinking about it all the time, it must be the right thing, don't you think so? Have you ever felt that strongly about something, Miss Student, that you just know it's right? That's the way I feel about this and I just can't wait to tell you what it is. You see, this big thing I've been trying to decide is I'm thinking about recommending you for Lifetime Membership. Before you say anything I want to caution you to keep it a secret. . . ."

The teacher explains the club's exclusiveness. "If you were ever turned down or disapproved, I know you would be very embarrassed. I certainly would. . . . But keep your fingers crossed . . . as far as I am concerned you have every requirement. Of course, I think so much of you I may have a biased opinion. However, Mr. Murray doesn't see you as I do. He doesn't know what a wonderful person you are, as I do, but I think we can convince him, don't you?"

The teacher goes on to explain that the student must be approved by the studio, by the manager, and, finally, by either the regional director or Arthur Murray. To begin with, the teacher must write a letter recommending the student, and the student must also write a letter, asking for acceptance into the Lifetime Club. The student and the teacher work on these letters together.[4] Only when this is done and the full benefits of the club have been described in glowing terms does the teacher mention the cost.

"I wish there was a club like this for teachers. Actually, I don't think they charge enough for it. It's a very low price to pay to have your social life taken care of for the rest of your life, don't you think so? Only $12,000 and you don't have to worry about a thing again. . . ."

If the student remarks that this sounds like a great deal of money, the teacher has an answer memorized to shame her into retracting the thought.

"I hope I didn't hear that right, that you would set a monetary value on something like this. Please don't dis-

[4] The teacher has a whole manual of form letters at his disposal.

courage me or make me think I'm wrong because to have that much faith in someone I just couldn't be wrong. You are the type of person I think you are and you can't tell me any different."

In the series of playlets that are now acted out, first with the supervisor, then with the manager, and finally with the regional director or even with Arthur Murray himself, the teacher always acts as the student's friend. He is like a carnival shill egging on a country boy to try his hand at crown and anchor, or—and here the parallel is more telling—he is the Steer man in the Payoff, bringing the Egg to meet the Player.[5] There have been a host of variations and refinements, depending on the studio and the participants, but the basic method is the same.

First the student is propelled by the teacher into the presence of the supervisor. The supervisor expresses surprise and pleasure as she reads the letters of application. Indeed, to use a phrase from one manual, she is "overcome."

"We always felt you were a wonderful student, Miss Jones, but I had no idea you felt this way. This certainly is a surprise." After some further byplay, it is explained to the student that the manager and the regional director must also approve. Meanwhile, however, the sale is written up and signed, and the financing arranged.

"Pupils rarely have $12,000 sitting idle in the bank," the Toronto manual explains. "They usually have stocks and bonds and matured insurance policies. . . . The Supervisor should find out diplomatically just how pupil has money invested. . . . If pupil says 'I think I can afford it,' say 'Go home and think. We cannot go to the Regional Director unless all these things are right.' You still haven't asked them.

---

[5] The difference, of course, is that Murray students do get something for their money.

You don't give them a chance to say NO. They can't go around the Studio saying: 'I was offered a Lifetime, but I refused' as this would lower the prestige of the Club. . . ."

It may be that the teacher has not been able to persuade the student to write a letter. No matter; the two of them will visit the supervisor anyway, under the pretext of "getting more information." In such cases the supervisor is a little cooler. A procedure developed by a successful Arthur Murray studio in Albany, New York, is often used here. The supervisor says he feels the whole thing is a "little premature in my mind"—the pupil must have a sponsor, first of all. The teacher eagerly announces that he will act as sponsor. The supervisor explains that the student must write a letter to Arthur Murray himself and the sponsor must write one, too. These must be strong letters to convince Mr. Murray that the pupil is of Lifetime caliber.

The teacher and pupil leave, and the teacher continues the sales talk, urging the pupil to write her letter that night. The following day he has this to say: "When I went home last night and started to write my letter sponsoring you, I got so excited I couldn't sleep. If this didn't go through for you, I'd be just sick. The more I wrote about why you deserve the Lifetime, the more determined I became to do everything I can to get it for you."

The technique developed in Albany was to have this letter rejected as not good enough. This form of "fear selling" was also adopted by the Toronto studio. At this point the reluctant student's pride was hurt and the prize of a Lifetime, dangled just ahead of his nose, seemed more desirable as it grew unattainable. The second letter, of course, was accepted.

The sixth step of the original Toronto procedure was for the supervisor, the teacher, and the student to visit the manager.

The Manager should be very surprised but non-committal until he has read all the letters and made comment on a few things.

The manager, after some thought, says he thinks the student is deserving and he will send the letter along to Arthur Murray.

The teacher knows exactly what to do at this point since he has acted out the exact playlet in sales meetings. He becomes excited and asks the manager to call Arthur Murray (or the regional director) on the phone; otherwise he will be a nervous wreck waiting for the answer. The manager allows himself to be swayed, but first he says to the pupil: "Once I present this, it is up to him. If he says NO, that's it. He will probably want to speak to you, Miss Jones, so have it clear in your mind what you want to say."

If the student at this point shows signs of panic, all three staff members know what to do to keep her from raising possible objections. They rehearse her in the phone call that is to follow. ("It is positive action that keeps them from other things," staff members are reminded.) As this is going on and the call is being put through, the manager is preparing the legal documents. The instructions to the teacher regarding the phone conversation that follows speak for themselves.

Have your call put through. Be really excited when you talk to Mr. Murray. Tell him about your wonderful pupil. Read the letters and your comments, then say: "Yes, Mr. Murray, she definitely can afford it" (nodding your head YES and looking at the pupil). "No, Mr. Murray, it won't crimp her" (shaking your head NO and looking at the pupil). "Yes, Mr.Murray, she is coming in four hours per week, but she is planning to come in more per week" (going through the same motions).

The pupil talks briefly on the phone and then pandemonium breaks out.

This is the big moment. Teacher, Supervisor and Manager are all jumping around congratulating the pupil. Manager has her sign the enrolment and gets cheque. Teacher and Supervisor should rush out to the ballroom with the pupil and stop the music. Announce that Miss Pupil has just . . . been approved for Lifetime Membership. Teacher and pupil do a short exhibition. Then every teacher should grab their pupil and rush over and congratulate pupil. She is literally "Queen for a Day." This gives the other teachers an opening to discuss Lifetime Memberships with their pupils.[6]

And is this the end of the subtle sales propaganda as far as Miss Pupil is concerned? Not necessarily: for the Murray system of dancing is ingeniously arranged so that it has been possible for students to buy more than one Lifetime Membership. There has been an even higher status known as a Double Lifetime Membership. A special technique for selling it was also developed.

Mr. and Mrs. Blank, you were the first couple to become Lifetime Members so I think you should know about this. We have another couple here and I have heard, through the grapevine, that they wanted to apply for a Double Membership. In fact, they are going to apply next week

[6] It goes without saying that the procedure here varies depending upon the eagerness of the student to join. If the student is a drooling prospect, many of these steps are eliminated. In the interests of brevity, I have telescoped much of the procedure. The Lifetime applicant, for instance, must also pass three separate boards—a dance board, a student board, and a final "closing" board. The student board consists of Lifetime members, who may, theoretically, blackball an applicant; this has rarely occurred in practice.

and I think that you should have the opportunity to be the first couple to be approved for Double Membership.

In Arthur Murrayland, then, there seems to be no end to selling, any more than there can be an end to dancing. As the students twist and tango on through life—through several Lives, perhaps—dancing and salesmanship, and, indeed, existence itself, become inexorably entwined. Ballroom and salesroom merge into one and none can say where the dance leaves off and the pitch begins. The first free lesson has been transformed into a way of life, and the seductive flattery of the other actors in the drama is as needful to the spirit as the music of the dance itself.

The customer pays cheerfully, via the installment system, for his weekly portion of Black Magic. Mesmerized he well may be, but he has bought himself a place of sorts in the unfriendly world. Who can say that he has not been given his money's worth?

9

You, Too, Can Be a Hard Head

"Do not waste time on hard heads at the door," Collier's instruction manual warns would-be encyclopaedia salesmen. It is good advice. A hard head is sales proof. There is no reasoning with him. He will not succumb to blandishments about the health of his children, the free advertising program, the boys' trip to Europe, or even his need to fulfill himself through dancing. In the salesman's lexicon the hard head is a sneak and a blackguard, an enemy of the free-enterprise system, and, therefore, a villain of the deepest dye. Yet it can be argued that there are advantages in being hard-headed. (The phrase, after all, has been applied to top executives of some of the very companies which engage in the witchery described in this book.) Is it not better to be a hard head than a soft head?

It has perhaps occurred to some readers, especially those who have studied the methods of the hard-headed Operative 67, that the very techniques which salesmen use to lure customers can be employed to thwart salesmen. Surely, if salesmen can memorize certain gambits, the hard heads can devise opposing ploys. If a salesman has at his fingertips a script that teaches him how to overcome objections, a hard head can also be armed with a manual that tells him how to overcome a salesman who tries to overcome objections. If the sales technique is to force the prospect to agree with the salesman, surely the hard-head technique is to force the salesman to agree with *him*.

SALESMAN: (*quoting from memorized script*): If there was a way in which your wife could own this gold-plated olive mincer at no excessive cost, you'd certainly want her to have it—now isn't that right, Mr. Jones?

HARD HEAD: No! Our kitchen is cluttered up with too many gadgets as it is. I'm sure you agree with Christ's teachings that material possessions are only a burden to anyone seeking spiritual regeneration. Isn't that right, Mr. Smith?

SALESMAN: Well, I——

HARD HEAD: (*pressing advantage*): Well, *isn't* it? The Bible teaches that. What are you —some kind of an atheist or something?

My friend George Feyer, the celebrated television cartoonist, is perhaps the most ingenious hard head that I know. He is Hungarian by birth and brings to the art of hard-headedness that special flair which distinguishes so many of his countrymen. Prospective hard heads may wish to commit to memory the essentials of three of his more imaginative gambits.

GAMBIT NO. 1: THE SUSPICIOUS TECHNIQUE

SALESMAN: Good afternoon, sir, I represent the Family Counselling Division of the National Home Service League.

FEYER: Is that a Communist front organization?

SALESMAN: *Wh-at?*

FEYER: I am in a sensitive industry and I have to be careful. Have you been cleared for security?

SALESMAN: Well, just a minute. My company's one of the largest——

FEYER: How do I know that? There are spies everywhere. Freedom's arsenal is a vigilant America. Don't you agree?

SALESMAN: Why, yes, but——

FEYER: You bring your security clearance along, properly stamped and counter-signed, and we'll talk again. . . .

GAMBIT NO. 2: THE SELF-ASSURED TECHNIQUE

SALESMAN: If it was possible for us to place this encyclopaedia in your home, absolutely free, Mr. Feyer, would you agree to keep it up to date?

FEYER: No, I wouldn't. I don't need an encyclopaedia. I know everything.

SALESMAN: Oh, *come* now, sir——

FEYER: Are you calling me a liar? Ask me anything. Want to know the length of the Nile? It's 4,050 miles from its ultimate headstream, the Kegira, to the delta at the Mediterranean. You want to know how much territory it drains? One million one hundred thousand square miles. What's the descent between Khartoum and Aswan? Come on—I bet you don't know that. Do you know that figure?

SALESMAN: Now, just a moment——

FEYER: You see, you're not educated. You're the one who needs an encyclopaedia. Why don't you get them to place one in your home? No man can call himself a whole human being unless he has at his fingertips an impeccable reference work which can bring him up to date about the world he lives in —don't you agree?

GAMBIT NO. 3: THE "INSIDERS" TECHNIQUE

SALESMAN: Good afternoon, I'm from the advertising department of Genuine Cookwares, Ltd., and we're taking a survey——

FEYER: Advertising man, eh? You must know Joe Hanson down there.

SALESMAN: Joe—*Hanson?*

FEYER: He handles all the General Cookwares advertising. I work with him. You must know him.

SALESMAN: You work with him?

FEYER: Sure, I'm one of their top people. I get all the cookware I want at cost (chuckle). I'm up to my neck in cook-

> ware. Say, what's wrong? I thought
> you were going to survey me. . . .

Feyer's many gambits, of which this is only a sampling (there is another in which he tells the salesman he actually *makes* the product that is being sold), have emboldened me to devise some further techniques in hard-headedness. Generally speaking, the hard head can adopt one of two attitudes: *the high-minded attitude* or *the slob attitude*. I have listed my examples under these headings.

THE HIGH-MINDED ATTITUDE

Example One: A Bible salesman tries to overcome an objection from a prospect who says she already owns a Bible.

SALESMAN: I was sure, Mrs. Jones, that a person of your character would have several Bibles in her home. Just think, though, how much more beautiful and understandable *this* masterpiece is. (*He shows $50 illustrated Bible.*)

HARD HEAD: Yes, Mr. Smith, the pictures *are* lovely, but I know that a person as fine as you wouldn't want to go against another's religious beliefs. You see, our sect doesn't believe the word of God should be tampered with. The simple words of the Good Book, unadorned by sinful pictures or expensive worldly trappings are quite good enough for us. I'm sure you'll agree, Mr. Smith, that the Word of God needs no adornment. Isn't that true?

SALESMAN: But don't you agree that——

233

HARD HEAD: (*swiftly and smoothly*): Don't *you* agree, Mr. Smith, that the extra money would be better spent among the heathen peoples of Mozambique?

Example Two: An encyclopaedia salesman tries to get a prospect to "qualify."

SALESMAN: We'd like to place this library with your family as a premium in return for permission to use your name. . . .

HARD HEAD: Oh, that's very flattering, but I'm afraid my position in the community makes it impossible for me to take advantage of your offer.

SALESMAN: Don't get me wrong, Mr. Jones, we won't publish your name. It's not an endorsement. It's simply a statement of ownership—like a library list.

HARD HEAD: Oh, I quite realize that. But, you see, it's part of my philosophy that I never use my personal status to advance my own position commercially. Don't you agree the world would be a finer place if people were less selfish?

SALESMAN: Well, now, it's not a question of selfishness, surely.

HARD HEAD: Oh, yes, it is. I would be getting something free in return for my good name. You said so yourself. It would be shoddy of me. No; I'm sorry I can't allow my name to be cheapened in this way.

Example Three: A mixing-machine salesman tells a house-wife the device is absolutely free if she buys a supply of milk powder.

HARD HEAD: You mean your company is going to give me this wonderful machine absolutely free?

SALESMAN: That's correct, Mrs. Jones.

HARD HEAD: Oh, I couldn't accept it, Mr. Smith. It's part of our family code that we don't take charity.

SALESMAN: Oh, well, now, it isn't charity, Mrs. Jones. After all, we are asking for something in return. Your opinions on this survey. . . .

HARD HEAD: Oh, I know, you're being very kind in order to salve my pride and I appreciate it. I guess somebody must have told you how badly off we are. And it was certainly nice of you not to want to hurt my feelings. But our family stands on its own feet, Mr. Smith; we just cannot accept something for nothing; we wouldn't be able to live with ourselves if we did. Don't you think that the human race would be better off if everybody stood on his own two feet? As a thinking man, wouldn't you agree with that?

SALESMAN: Well, perhaps, but surely——

HARD HEAD: Why don't you just give the machine to the Salvation Army, Mr. Smith?

I must warn the reader that these gambits require considerable experience on the part of those who use them. That is why, for beginning hard heads, I recommend the slob attitude. Though it lacks the delicacy of the more refined technique, its meat-ax approach is undeniably effective.

THE SLOB ATTITUDE

Example One: An ingenuous-looking young magazine salesman knocks on the door.

SALESMAN: Hello, there: you're Mrs. Jones? Gee, I hope I didn't take you away from anything. My name's John Doe and I just dropped by to get your approval on the boys' tour of Europe.

HARD HEAD: Well, I don't approve of boys touring around Europe. I don't know what their mothers are thinking of, I'm sure. Traipsing about those foreign countries when they ought to be home studying and doing chores. I declare I'd whomp any kid of mine tried to trek off to Europe. That's how Communism spreads, son.

Example Two: An encyclopaedia salesman arrives at the qualifying question.

SALESMAN: Don't you agree, Mr. Jones, that if this valuable ten-volume reference library were to be placed in your home, your family would benefit by years of education?

HARD HEAD: Who wants an education? I had none and I done good. Don't talk to me about education! Where's it got us anyway—all this science talk and psychology? In the soup, that's where.

Are we any better off, any happier for
an education? Not one bit, Mac. As
far's I'm concerned, the less education
my kids get the better. Stuffin' their
heads with a lot of nonsense, that's all
it is. Isn't that right?

Example Three: The mixing-machine salesman talks glibly
about the need for healthy children.

SALESMAN: You are interested in better nutrition
and health for your family if it's possible to get it, aren't you, Mrs. Jones?
HARD HEAD: No.
SALESMAN: *No?*
HARD HEAD: They're too healthy now. They're running me ragged. I'm going to start
feeding them less. They've had too
many vitamins, that's the trouble.
They're going to burn themselves out.
SALESMAN: But surely you want them to be properly fed?
HARD HEAD: That's been the problem—too *much*
food. I'm cutting them right off milk
next week, soon's I use up the box of
crystals. Maybe that'll help quiet my
husband down nights. When he has
too much nutrition there's no holding
him back.

It is probably unnecessary to give further examples, since
ingenious hard heads can while away many a dull winter's
afternoon devising techniques of their own. A few general
suggestions might be useful, however.

TEN BASIC RULES FOR HARD HEADS

1. *Always try to sell something of your own to the salesman.* If he's peddling encyclopaedias, for instance, bring out an old set and give him a sales talk about it. If you haven't one of your own, tell him you have a friend who wants to sell one. Always try to sell a vacuum-cleaner salesman *your* vacuum cleaner. Insist on demonstrating it. Take lots of time.

2. *Survey the surveyors.* If the salesman says he is taking a survey for the advertising department, tell him that *you* belong to a survey organization. Have a form already prepared for him to fill in. Insist on asking him about his hobbies, his favorite TV programs, his smoking habits, his insurance plan, and his opinions regarding nuclear testing.

3. *Interrupt all sales talks with irrelevant questions.* When money is mentioned, for instance, ask what bank the company deals with. Insist on knowing the manager's name. Ask if the salesman knows him personally. Be interested in your salesman. Ask intelligent questions about his family background. Take plenty of time.

4. *Tell funny stories.* Have a fund of old jokes on hand so that whenever the salesman makes a point you can cut in with: "Say, that reminds me of a good one. . . ." Tell him you have to make a speech to a local church group. Insist on rehearsing it in front of him. Ask him for his opinions. If he balks, look hurt and say: "You asked me for *my* opinions. Turn about is fair play, surely."

5. *Put the salesman to work.* Be a helpless householder. Get him to help you move the piano. Ask him if he'd mind watching the baby while you go across the street to borrow some sugar. Explain that you have to bathe the children and ask if he'd mind demonstrating his wares

while you're doing that. Make him hold the soap. Splash water on him.

6. *Insist on thorough demonstrations.* This applies especially to demonstrations of mixing machines, vacuum cleaners, floor polishers, and other labor-saving devices. Make sure the salesman cleans the entire house before you reject the device. Have him clean the front-room carpet while you and your friends enjoy a small, intimate dinner.

7. *Form a Hard-Head Club in your neighborhood.* When the salesman leaves, tell him you feel sorry for him. Tell him you have a list of friends who would be excellent prospects for him. Then give him a list of club members in good standing. Award points, bonuses, and prizes to club members who come up with new sales-resistance techniques. Print details of personal experiences in the club bulletin.

8. *Sabotage mail-order companies by filling out all FREE TRIAL coupons.* Use names and addresses of friends, enemies, casual acquaintances, or simply names taken from the telephone directory. Send in as many as possible. Get fellow hard heads to pledge that they will never pay for or acknowledge free trial books, magazines, vitamins, courses, or other material sent in this way. Explain that a free trial coupon is not a legal document and thus the company cannot make good its legal threats. Give bonuses to members who collect the largest number of threatening letters.

9. *Ship unsolicited mail-order material back to the sender with insufficient postage.* Arrange for your hard-heads club to launch a monthly drive whereby tons of brochures are sent back, first class, through the mails, without postage. If material carries return postage, always remove it.

10. *Have a Club Dance Night every third Thursday.* Collect free dance-lesson certificates, then visit your nearest dance studio *en masse.* Insist on giving dance instruction to the instructors. Explain you despise dancing and have no intention of carrying on but can't resist anything that's free. Ask to be shown a Lifetime member. Present the impoverished Lifetime member with a charity hamper of nourishing foods. Sing the club song before departing.

I must explain that these rules are designed only for that minority which thrives on excitement, enjoys living dangerously, and is prepared for a strenuous clash of wills. The game, as outlined here, is not unlike the hazardous teen-age contest known as Chicken.

The experienced hard head will not play Chicken with salesmen; he has learned that any prolonged contact with the breed can be as dangerous as contact with a typhoid carrier. The successful hard head is, after all, a cautious man who has discovered that there is only one sure defense against his adversaries. In the unending seesaw battle between the public and those who practice the big sell, the hard heads who survive are the ones who have enough gumption to slam the door.

A NOTE ABOUT THE AUTHOR

PIERRE BERTON has long been fascinated by human folly, as was evident in his hitherto most successful book, *The Klondike Fever* (1958). Among his other books for the general reader are *The Mysterious North* (1956) and *The Royal Family* (1954). He has also written two books for younger readers, *Stampede for Gold* (1955) and *The Secret World of Og* (Atlantic Press, 1962). He was born in the Klondike region of Canada and spent his boyhood there. At twenty-one he became city editor of the Vancouver *News Herald* and, after various other newspaper jobs, managing editor of *Maclean's* magazine. For many years he wrote a widely read column for the *Toronto Star,* and he appears regularly on Canadian television programs, and occasionally on U.S. programs. He lives near Toronto with his wife and six children.

A NOTE ON THE TYPE

THE TEXT of this book is set in CALEDONIA, a Linotype face designed by W. A. Dwiggins (1880–1956), the man responsible for so much that is good in contemporary book design and typography. Caledonia belongs to the family of printing types called "modern face" by printers —a term used to mark the change in style of type-letters that occurred about 1800. Caledonia borders on the general design of Scotch Modern but is more freely drawn than that letter.